CAMBRIDGE LIBRARY COLLECTION

Books of enduring scholarly value

Travel and Exploration

The history of travel writing dates back to the Bible, Caesar, the Vikings and the Crusaders, and its many themes include war, trade, science and recreation. Explorers from Columbus to Cook charted lands not previously visited by Western travellers, and were followed by merchants, missionaries, and colonists, who wrote accounts of their experiences. The development of steam power in the nineteenth century provided opportunities for increasing numbers of 'ordinary' people to travel further, more economically, and more safely, and resulted in great enthusiasm for travel writing among the reading public. Works included in this series range from first-hand descriptions of previously unrecorded places, to literary accounts of the strange habits of foreigners, to examples of the burgeoning numbers of guidebooks produced to satisfy the needs of a new kind of traveller - the tourist.

China Under the Search-Light

A London-born Wesleyan Methodist missionary, William Arthur Cornaby (1860–1921) spent over thirty years in China, where he edited *The Chinese Christian Review*, and, from 1905, the *Ta Tung Pao*, a weekly magazine targeted at Chinese officials and scholars. His many books on Chinese culture and civilisation, including *A String of Chinese Peach-Stones* (1895) and *Rambles in Central China* (1896), provide detailed sketches of Chinese rural life and customs. The later *China Under the Search-Light,* first published in 1901, uses Western clichés about China as a point of departure to offer a more nuanced understanding of the underlying facts and problems specific to Chinese society. In this book, Cornaby discusses contemporary topics such as overcrowding in Shanghai, mandarins, and Buddhism. He also scrutinises newspapers, novels, and aesthetic traditions, offering an elementary introduction to Chinese culture as perceived by a nineteenth-century British missionary.

T0381747

Cambridge University Press has long been a pioneer in the reissuing of out-of-print titles from its own backlist, producing digital reprints of books that are still sought after by scholars and students but could not be reprinted economically using traditional technology. The Cambridge Library Collection extends this activity to a wider range of books which are still of importance to researchers and professionals, either for the source material they contain, or as landmarks in the history of their academic discipline.

Drawing from the world-renowned collections in the Cambridge University Library, and guided by the advice of experts in each subject area, Cambridge University Press is using state-of-the-art scanning machines in its own Printing House to capture the content of each book selected for inclusion. The files are processed to give a consistently clear, crisp image, and the books finished to the high quality standard for which the Press is recognised around the world. The latest print-on-demand technology ensures that the books will remain available indefinitely, and that orders for single or multiple copies can quickly be supplied.

The Cambridge Library Collection will bring back to life books of enduring scholarly value (including out-of-copyright works originally issued by other publishers) across a wide range of disciplines in the humanities and social sciences and in science and technology.

China
Under the
Search-Light

WILLIAM ARTHUR CORNABY

CAMBRIDGE
UNIVERSITY PRESS

CAMBRIDGE UNIVERSITY PRESS

Cambridge, New York, Melbourne, Madrid, Cape Town, Singapore,
São Paolo, Delhi, Dubai, Tokyo

Published in the United States of America by Cambridge University Press, New York

www.cambridge.org
Information on this title: www.cambridge.org/9781108014113

© in this compilation Cambridge University Press 2010

This edition first published 1901
This digitally printed version 2010

ISBN 978-1-108-01411-3 Paperback

CHINA UNDER THE SEARCH-LIGHT

CHINA UNDER THE SEARCH-LIGHT By

Wm. Arthur Cornaby, Editor
of the *Chung-si-chiao-hui-pao*, Author of
" A String of Chinese Peach-Stones," etc.

LONDON

T. FISHER UNWIN

PATERNOSTER SQUARE

1901

Chapters ii–vii *and* ix *are reprinted from the*
"*North China Herald.*"

CONTENTS

—◦◦◦—

CONTENTS

CHAPTER V.

DEAD-LEVELS.

CHAPTER VI.

RUTS.

CHAPTER VII.

THE "NATIVE FOREIGNER."

CONTENTS

CHAPTER XII.

A CHINESE BOOKSTALL.

CHAPTER XIII.

A DAILY NEWSPAPER.

An extraordinary feature in the history of manners is the utter disability of people to judge of the manners of other nations . . . with fairness and common sense. An English lady turns away her face with disgust when she sees Oriental women with bare feet and legs; while the Eastern ladies are horrified at the idea of women in Egypt walking about bare-faced. Admirers of Goethe may get over the idea that this great poet certainly ate fish with a knife; but when we are told that Beatrice never used a fork, and that Dante never changed his linen for weeks, some of our illusions are rudely disturbed.—*Max Muller, " Chips."*

All within the four seas are brethren.—*Ancient proverb, cited by Confucius* (551–479 B.C.).

INTRODUCTORY CHAPTER

In his *Study of Sociology* Herbert Spencer tells a tale of a Frenchman " who, having been three weeks in England, proposed to write a book on English characteristics, who after three months found that he was not quite ready, and who, after three years, concluded that he knew nothing about it." We can vouch for the accuracy of the tale, except that the hero did not happen to be a Frenchman visiting England, but was an Englishman or American visiting China. We have known him well. He went there as globe-trotter, remained awhile as visitor, and lastly made up his mind to become a resident of the Far Eastern paradise of puzzles and problems.

3

Let us study him awhile and inquire how it came to pass that his enthusiasm for printer's ink met with such a remarkable collapse.

The explanation is that travel reveals the differences between one race and another—differences which are chiefly external and concern such things as Carlyle would sum up in the one word *clothes*. While residence reveals the similarities beneath all externals—the essential human characteristics common to mankind the wide world over. Add to this that Far Eastern races produce the illusion of similarity of feature in the traveller's mind, whose most frequent remark is that " the Chinese are all alike." This being so, the external strangeness as compared with his own land invites the snap-shotter, and the apparent sameness of feature and disposition among the natives themselves provokes his faculties of generalisation. Thus he is apt to rush into print.

But as he lengthens his stay and becomes a resident, the common human nature of the Chinese race impresses him; and a great divergency of feature and disposition becomes apparent between one native and another. The first item tends to overpower his initial sense of national difference, while the personal divergencies of character among his native acquaintances make it more and more difficult to generalise upon them. He cannot see the wood for the trees.

In dealing with the Chinese, moreover, he is dealing with the inhabitants of a continent rather than of a country. The men of Shantung and Shansi in the north may differ widely from those of more central China, and these again may differ in character as much as they do in speech from the Cantonese. To the careful observer, indeed, the features of a Hunanese will be seen to differ in a marked manner from those of a man from Szchuan in the west, so much so that he may generally identify the natives of either province from a mere glance at their faces.

Then the Chinese naturally divide themselves into the four classes of scholars, farmers, artizans, and traders—naturally, not only from their differing occupations, but also from their differing characteristics of disposition. The literati, for instance, are trained to an outward suavity of bearing, to the wearing of a conventional mask, which the rest have hardly learned to assume with any constancy of habit.

Thus, to sum up, it may often be easy to gain totally different answers to many a simple question about China: concerning the climate, for one part lies within the tropics and another is subject to the severest winters; concerning the food of the people, for in the north flour rather than rice is the chief item of daily cookery; concerning modes of transit, for there are comparatively broad roads in northern

China where one may hire a cart or even a camel, while the "roads" of Mid-China differ little from field-paths, and the barrow and sedan-chair are the only vehicles obtainable by the traveller. The men of China may be correctly described as adepts at artifice, and also with almost equal correctness as of comparatively transparent dispositions (the latter being true of many a countryman) ; as buying and selling only after a prolonged process of haggling over prices, and of having but one price for all alike (as in the case of many a merchant and larger shop-keeper). The women may be described as universally binding their feet (as in several provinces), or of reserving that genteel mode of early torture for the more fashionable and wealthy (as in some southern provinces). It may also be affirmed that the idols of China out-number the inhabitants (in certain parts), and also that in a score of households hardly one idol is to be found (in other regions). So that reliable generalisations may be exceedingly difficult to make on many a point which seems so obvious to the chance visitor to any one given region.

But should certain events transpire, such as an anti-foreign rising, which will throw up the national characteristics into contrast with those of the West, affording the resident a certain amount of aloofness, and placing him at a mental distance sufficient to gain a true perspective of the whole, then all the varied items of information which his familiarity with Chinese life and thought has placed at his disposal will be a help and not a hindrance to an attempt at national portraiture.

And what, we may ask, are the essential conditions of familiarity (say) with British characteristics on the part of a Frenchman? Surely a grasp of the language, so that he can speak it, think in it, read and write it with more or less ease, and residence in the country until he ceases to be known as "that foreigner," but becomes known by name as Monsieur So-and-So.

Read *China* instead of *England*, and *Hsien-sheng* (Signor) instead of *Monsieur*, and we have some of the essential conditions of familiarity with China. To which may be added the eschewing of "foreign" steamers and the adoption of small native boats or of travel on foot in company with a native friend, until stress of experiences common to both men shall result in much community of feeling.

As sources of reliable information on popular manners may be mentioned country folk, merchants, native Christians, tale-books, and the National Records. And as sources of most unreliable information— highly commended to those who merely wish to retain their preconceived notions— Chinese guests on their society behaviour, and above all mandarins, especially those connected with the Court, whose profession it is to put the unwary foreigner off the scent.   These latter Chinese or Manchu gentry might, with the sole alteration of the one word in brackets, adopt as their motto the confession of Nello the barber in George Eliot's *Romola* : " We (Florentines) have liberal ideas about speech, and consider that an instrument which can flatter and promise so cleverly as the tongue must have been partly made for the purpose ; and that truth is a riddle for eyes and wits to discover, which it were a mere spoiling of sport for the tongue to betray."

Over the whole of Chinese officialdom floats the yellow banner, whose device represents the dragon in the act of swallowing the Japanese sun, which is "quartered" on the flag just as the crosses of St. Andrew and St. Patrick are incorporated in the Union Jack.   Some centuries ago the Chinese dragon fully intended to swallow the Japanese sun.   The attempt was markedly unsuccessful, but that is a mere detail, and the national banner was henceforth modified as though the deed had been done. Which thing is suggestive of much.

In the following chapters it is proposed to start with a few sights which will be familiar to the most hurried visitor to Shanghai—such as a dense population, a countryman staring at some Western wonder, a Chinese urchin smoking a cigarette, a missionary in Chinese dress, a mandarin and his retinue, an elegant Chinese signboard, a bookstall and a native newspaper— to start with such familiar sights, and to throw the searching light of careful study upon the facts and problems behind each of them.

For the benefit of the many readers who have not taken a trip to Shanghai a description of that "model settlement" may be given here. The picture has been drawn by a distinguished author and critic so graphically as to save the resident the trouble of endeavouring to revive his first impressions in order to attempt a picture of his own.

"Among the many surprises of a journey to the Far East," says Henry Norman, "one of the greatest is certainly the first sight of Shanghai. . . . I could hardly believe my eyes. There lay a magnificent European city surrounding a broad and crowded river. True, the magnificence is only skin-deep ; all the architectural beauty and solidity of Shanghai being along the river ; but I am speaking of the first impressions of Shanghai, and in this re-spect it is superior to New York, far ahead of San Francisco, and almost as imposing for the moment as Liverpool itself. A broad and beautifully kept boulevard, called, of course, ' The Bund,' runs round the river, with rows of well-grown trees and a broad grass-plat at the water's edge, and this Bund is lined on the other side from one end to the other with mercantile buildings second to none of their kind in the world. . . . At the upper end of the Bund a large patch of green shows the Public Gardens, where the band plays on summer evenings. All night all Shanghai is bright with the electric light, and its telegraph poles remind you of Chicago. . . . And the needed touch of colour is added to the scene as you look at it from on deck, by the gay flags of the steamers and the Consular bunting floating over the town."

The Prince of the State of Ch'i sent a courtier with a missive to the Queen Dowager of Chao, who, without breaking the seal, inquired, saying: "Have the crops been good? And are the populace well? And is the Prince well?" Whereat the messenger was not pleased, and said, "Your Majesty asks not after the Prince, but first after the crops and the people! Is that not placing the mean first and the honourable last?" But the Queen replied, "Not so, for were there no crops, how could there be any populace? And were there no populace, how could there be any Prince?"—*History of the Contending States*, (Anon.), 3rd Century B.C.

CHAPTER II

THE over-density of China's populations is
sure to be one of the first facts which strike
the traveller, and the words "Yellow
Peril" to form the first jotting in his
notebook. From his earliest days, he has
been taught to realise that "if the inhabitants of China could be made to march
before us at the rate of sixty per minute
every day and night, under the sunlight
and the solemn stars, the endless procession
would move on for twelve years and eight
months," and that the fact of the Chinese
nation being estimated at four hundred
millions involves a death-rate of a million
per month. And here he sees it all before

him in sample, and instinctively recalls a picture of "Over-population" in Cruikshank's *Comic Almanac*. But being of a thoughtful turn of mind, it is not the comicality of the scene before him, but the peril of it all to the world in years to come which impresses him. He can well believe that the Chinese are likely to overrun the world in time, that "twenty millions or more of Boxers . . . will make residence in China impossible for foreigners . . . and will carry the Chinese flag and Chinese arms into many a place that even fancy will not suggest to-day, thus preparing for the future upheavals and disasters never even dreamt of." And he shudders for his grandchildren, whom he pictures as swept away by such tremendous centrifugal forces.

And all this seems easily feasible. But the question arises as to whether the opening up of China will not rather mean the birth of a centripetal force, which will check the tendency toward emigration (except among inhabitants of China's coasts), especially among a people who are naturally home-staying, and who are not addicted, as their proverb has it, to "reject the near for the distant" when the means of livelihood are to be found close at hand.

And in this connection some remarkable statistics and inferences by that most accurate and accomplished sinologue, Dr. Ernst Faber, may serve to mitigate many a fear. He points out that it is only the river-basins that are over-populated; that the average population of Germany is three times denser than the average population of China, and that the Chinese Empire ought to be able comfortably to support at least five times its present inhabitants.

The more intricate question of the Boxers will be dealt with at length from its historical side in Chapter viii., and the reader may well pluck heart from the consideration that under the most diligent fostering from the

3

Manchu Court, the movement which has given us the term " Boxer " only infested a mere tenth of China Proper. Such fostering forces will thus have to be multiplied by ten and become continuous for at least two years, as in the genesis of the Boxers, in order to bring about a really national movement for the extermination of the foreigner.

As a factor in the evolution of national character, the density of the population deserves a more extended notice. It is a leading element in nearly all regions of China where the merchant and missionary have penetrated. And, strange as it may seem, it is in the country places, rather than the towns and cities, that the overcrowding is most apparent. Take an average tract of farm land in England as seen from the windows of a railway carriage, and compare it with an average tract of farm land in China, up-country, a score of miles from the banks of the rivers Yangtse and Han,

and we find that in place of the solitary
English homestead China exhibits a dozen
little hamlets, which were indeed solitary
homesteads once, but which have grown
with the growth of the family or clan
through the years into clusters of ten or
more cottages. Thus if a walk through
any Chinese town calls forth the question,
" How do all these folks manage to live ? "
a ramble through such country parts can
but emphasise the question.

The immediate explanation is supplied by
the fact that where the best farm land of
England yields but one crop a year, and
may have to lie fallow every now and then,
the Chinese farmer expects at least two
crops, and in well-watered regions three
crops, from his, and no more feels the
necessity of letting the land lie fallow than
he does personally of resting from drudgery
one day in seven. He has no word in his
vocabulary for fallow ground, and no
amount of explanation will suffice to im-

press upon a Chinese farmer the rationale
of the process. Every available scrap of
decaying vegetable or animal produce is
thrown upon the land; and probably the
vigour of the Chinese sun serves with these
aids to renew the stock of microbes in the
soil, which turn the absorbed nitrogen of
the air into food for the crops, in accord
with the modern theory of fertilisation.
And what the Chinese farmer neglects to do
voluntarily, probably Nature does for him
forcibly in the occasional years of flood or
drought—causing the land, enriched with
vegetable matter in the form of half-grown
crops, to lie fallow for a season now and
then.

But, spite of all such considerations, the
density of China's population is an obvious
fact which, with the stationary habits of its
peoples for many centuries, has largely
influenced the development of national
characteristics.

A natural result of such density of

population has been the struggle for life which is everywhere apparent, and a vast development of the utilitarian instincts of the Chinese—a large proportion of whom live on year by year in a hand-to-mouth fashion.

One of the commonest elements of social intercourse, when a resident receives native guests in his own house, is the fact that rich and poor alike are sure not only to admire the various appurtenances of his home, but to ask, " What is the use of this ? " and especially, " What may have been the price of that ? " Such a visit presents a golden opportunity for inquiring what they have long thirsted to know— " What is the precise use of your stiff collar and cuffs ? And how much did the material of your coat and underclothing cost per foot ? " And from your wedding presents down to the latest newspaper lying on your table, the great point is, " What did everything cost ? "

A journey into the country, when a countryman or two are pretty sure to ask for the privilege of going " one road " with you, yields the same result. It is no use trying to avoid the question by saying that you are not a hat-merchant or second-hand clothes dealer, or that you prefer not to sell your boots just now, as you may need them later on. The question of questions is re-iterated until you begin to adopt the method of making your companion guess for himself. " Well," he replies, " those leather boots cost a dollar at least, I should think "—note the bargaining instinct here —" but what did they *really* come to ? " And your reply raises you in his estimation to a definite place in the category of beings human, for in your statement of the appar-ently fabulous sum you gave for each, your Chinese companion will see the bargaining instinct to be well developed in your case no less than in his, and will respect you for being so much like himself after all.

One side-consideration from the above is that missionaries who go far inland may be almost forced to adopt the native dress, if for no other reason than that their whole time might otherwise be taken up in answering questions concerning their strangely concocted and fabulously expensive attire. But the main consideration forced upon us is the poverty of the masses, who mostly regard five cents. (or one penny farthing) as an ample outlay for daily rice, and who may be accustomed to substitute bran for rice during some months of a poor year.

The utilitarian instincts fostered by pressure of circumstances are responsible on the one hand for the simplicity of methods so characteristic among all classes of Chinese artizans, and on the other hand have brought down what stands in place of religion to a matter of " luck-pidgin " and little more.

The farmer or shop-keeper worships an

idol if he should be extravagant enough to
afford one, or bows before a slip of dis-
coloured red paper marked "Heaven, Earth,
Sovereign, Parents, Teachers," or before an
ancestral tablet, with just the "Three
Manys" in mind (many riches, many sons,
many years of life), and with a special
reference to the first of the three. It will
cause no offence whatever, only provoke an
assenting smile, to tell a shop-keeper in
Mid-China that he looks upon his idol as a
cheap shop-assistant, who for a very low
wage, expended on incense, crackers, and
candles, is supposed to bring him many
customers and much gain. And in country
places, during times of drought, the farmers
have been known to scold their idols, then
curse them, then abandon them to the sun-
rays till paint and varnish are blistered, as
a punishment for not having fulfilled the
one purpose for which they were bought
(for a well-remembered sum) and nourished
(with so much incense, at a certain known

rate per month). Truly, as a writer has said of degenerate Israel during a particular epoch, " They employ, not worship, their gods."

Thus it is a distinctly foreign idea, imported with difficulty, and subject to heavy Customs dues, that anywhere in the world there can be any sort of godliness which is not so much gain-seeking. A Mission hospital is admired with the exclamation, " What merit you are accumulating! "—for reward in this life. And every native who joins the Christian Church is asked, " How much does the foreigner give you month by month? " though the man in question may have subscribed liberally toward Mission expenses. And all this is quite natural to the average Chinese, given his small stock of ideas, collected in a narrow area of space, and not added to by records extending through time. For a Confucian expects to make his living by his studies, if only as schoolmaster, and Taoist and Buddhist priest-monks are fed by the patrons of their respective temples.

Said a Buddhist monk to me once, "I don't worship idols any more than you do, Mr. Foreigner!"

"Why are you here in this temple, you rogue, then?" asked the crowd.

"To bang the drum, and pummel the bell, and spread the mat, and light the incense for you folks. A man must live, mustn't he?" was the unabashed reply.

Another indirect result of the density of the population is the development of that keen perception of character for which the Chinese are famous. An all-important question in the mind of a buyer toward a small salesman is, "Is he a deceiver or not?" And an equally important question of the salesman toward the buyer is, "Is he deceivable or not?"—until the two questions have come to form part of the daily catechism of China's millions, and have assumed national proportions in China's intercourse with Western Powers. The education of the Chinese in artifice and diplomacy, based on a recognition of degrees of deceivableness in others, has been going on for ages. It had its genesis in a prehistoric visit of a pedlar to some old-world Chinese village.

Another outcome of the conditions brought about by the local density of the population in China is the undoubted operation of the law of Survival of the Fittest. The tendency has been for weaklings to perish in infancy, sometimes by infanticide, commonly from natural causes aided by such facts as the customary suckling of infants for three years, and the chaotic condition of Chinese medical science and practice. It is a general idea, for instance, that smallpox is one of the unavoidable ills to which infantile flesh is heir. "They all get it" is a frequent remark, in deprecation of the inordinate

" fuss " that Western residents seem to make about the matter. " Yes, and many die, but who can help that ? " is the reply to further questioning. In country places there are absolutely no precautionary measures adopted in the case of infectious diseases, and even the isolation of patients is undreamt of. Over the corpse of a relative, senior or junior, who has departed this life by means of some infectious malady, a woman may be seen kneeling and wailing, her face every now and then touching the body or its clothing, with little ones tugging at her jacket for their overdue mother's milk.

A certain standard of robustness is therefore necessary for the survival of the children of the populace, and a certain amount of smartness is needed for the townsman who would make a living. Hence the " fitness " of the survivors is of two kinds—it is either strength of muscle, or adeptness in artifice. The

former seems to predominate among the
masses, while the latter becomes characteristic of the hucksters of the street,
and also of the literati generally, not
excepting the mandarins, or literati in
office. And that the phenomenon of
" ways that are dark, and tricks that are
vain " has been largely fostered by the
general struggle for life, seems to be
evidenced by the fact that among the
bigger shop-keepers and merchants, whose
flourishing trade lifts them above the
ordinary level of struggling Chinese
humanity, there seems to be little or no
tendency toward anything other than
straightforwardness and commercial in-
tegrity.

Societies of a communistic formation are characterised
by a tendency to rely, not on self, but on the
community, on the group, family, tribe, clan,
public powers, &c. The populations of the East
are the most striking representatives of this type.
—*Ed. Demoulins, " Anglo-Saxon Superiority,"*
p. 50.

Our (Confucian) religion well knows Heaven's will; it
looks on all under heaven as one family, great
rulers as elder branches in their parents' clan,
great ministers as chief officers of this clan, and
the people at large as brothers of the same
parents; and it holds that all things should be
enjoyed in common. — *King Hsien-ho, at the
World's Parliament of Religions.*

CHAPTER III

THE communistic basis of Chinese life seems closely related to the subject of the previous chapter. For let any kind of yielding and cohesive substances be compressed together, and the result will be either one solid lump, or a number of smaller lumps fitting into one another. Which latter is the case among the populations of China.

It is not claimed that the literal compression of overcrowding is in itself alone responsible for the peculiar form of solidarity to be found in China. That phenomenon seems to have been brought about by three kinds of compression. First there has been through the ages a social compression together of larger or smaller communities for common defence. Then there has been the political compression together of family groups by the adoption of the policy advocated by Confucius. And lastly, the literal compression which we have already noted.

Our earliest authentic picture of China is that of a ruling tribe, geographically settled down in the midst of semi-Chinese and more or less aboriginal tribes. This ruling State occupied the north of the present province of Honan, and from its position among semi-dependent States, was naturally called the Middle Realm, a term which afterwards came to be applied to the whole region controlled by that State, hence the modern phrase " Middle Kingdom."

The inter-relatedness of these various States, commonly quoted as eighteen in number, seems at first to have been little more than that of inter-marriage among various chieftains, following their subju-

SOLIDARITY 33

gation by the ruling tribe. By and by,
however, owing to the prosperity of any
one tribe disturbing "the balance of power,"
the unifying policy of inter-marriage was
supplemented by numerous blood-covenants
and even Peace Congresses—whose sequel
might well serve to establish the fact that
human nature remains practically the same
through the centuries.

Speaking roughly, we have, in and around
the times of Confucius, a Far Eastern
Europe. The recurring situations are
remarkably similar to those of modern
Europe, although the methods of dealing
with those situations were distinctively
Chinese. On which latter point it may
be affirmed in passing, that modern Chinese
statesmen, who are supposed to learn their
morals from Confucius, do as a fact find
rather in the history of the times around
that of Confucius, a liberal education in artifice requisite to deal with Western Powers.
Western governments might do worse

4

than make it a *sine quâ non* of Consulship,
and perhaps of Ministerial office, that each
candidate should gain a familiarity with
that all-important period of Chinese history.
For hardly a trick of trade but may be found
there in specimen, unless it be that un-
precedented stroke of genius of the Empress
Dowager in the year A.D. 1900, in formulating
a plan of slaughtering all Foreign Ministers,
and of issuing an edict commanding all
Viceroys and Governors to " destroy by
fire every foreign building, and painfully-
exterminate every foreign official, merchant,
missionary, and the like "—so the Chinese
text ran—throughout the land!   Most rules
have exceptions, and perhaps such an exception as this may not be claimed to
invalidate the above description of the
Chinese statesman's Text-book of Diplomacy, the history of the Chou dynasty,
B.C. 1122–221.

To return to our main argument, the
" Divided States " of that epoch may be

taken as a Chinese edition of Europe, but
as far as their lessening allegiance to the
nominal Son of Heaven is concerned, to
Europe from the Middle Ages onwards,
where a common allegiance to the Pope
of Rome furnishes a parallel to the one
link of connection which existed in ancient
China prior to the advent of that Emperor
of unscrupulous daring, who brought about
a comparative unification of the land in the
year B.C. 221. And from what glimpses of
the populace which we gain between the
lines of the very eventful history of those
times, we also gather that their want of
cohesiveness was much like that of medieval
Germany as described by Merle D'Aubigne—
" a people to be taken separately and singly
[that is, in families]; they have seldom or
never hitherto formed into groups and
parties." Except, as we gather from other
writers, by Trade Guilds similar to those
established among our Anglo-Saxon forefathers from time immemorial.

The disturbed state of China in those early days and the frequent revolutions ever since would naturally tend towards combination among blood-relations. The lesson learned in times of disturbance—that no man can afford to stand alone—would be so ingrained in the national consciousness as to become an axiom persisting in the popular mind during times of comparative peace. And as a fact it has impressed itself on the national literature in the form of a score of stock phrases descriptive of the supreme value of united energy. While, on the other hand, the man who has to stand alone is depicted under the metaphor of "a house supported by a single pillar," rather than upon the customary framework to which the walls are afterwards added as mere after-thoughts, as in Chinese buildings.

Realising these early conditions of existence, we may well admire the consummate wisdom of Confucius in throwing his whole energy into the strengthening of

existing family ties, especially those connected with parents and seniors generally.

He lived in an age of disintegration when
" even in his own State the obligations
between prince and subject were forgotten ;
when charity and duty to one's neighbour
were fast passing away; and right feeling
all but gone." And his view of the case
may be paraphrased in the words : " If only
the family rather than the individual were
the unit ; if only the supreme duty of life
were unquestioning devotion to parents, and
the local ruler or distant sovereign were
regarded as the ' parent of the people '—as
he was literally when the realm was but a
clan—then would government be easy
indeed. And, moreover, if to the practice
of filial duties could be coupled obedience
to elder brothers, and ' all within the four
seas ' were realised to be brethren—as they
were when the original Chinese clan took
up its residence within the circle of four
lakes once—then neighbourly habits would

prevail." Such seem to have been the
thoughts which moulded the politico-moral
philosophy of him whom the Chinese call
the Master.

That in the energy of his one purpose he
coupled the worship of ancestors with the
worship of the Supreme (*Shang Ti*), now
depersonified and attenuated into luminous
mist ; and that he taught that " an upright
son should conceal his father's dishonesty,"
must be fully admitted ; but from his standpoint as magistrate or counsellor of Princes,
with the consolidation of the realm as his
one consideration, what could have been
wiser than such a policy as his ?

Thus, partly through the exigencies of
lawless times, partly through the influence
of Confucian tenets, and partly by mechanical modes of compression, it comes
to pass that the family is the unit in China,
and that the individual is commonly regarded as a mere fraction of that unit.

As an extension of the principle, near

neighbours too, who in country places would be more or less related to the clan, are regarded very much as semi-relatives in towns and cities. In old Judæa the word *neighbour* seems to have implied some sort of relationship, and so it is in China to-day. Where, indeed, the privilege of local option is still extant, and two or three neighbours may be requisitioned by authorities to veto the purchase of land by a foreigner, should he wish to settle near.

The solidarity of the Chinese, then, seems to stop short at the family or cluster of neighbours, but within those narrow limits is a matter of daily observation. Is there a male birth, the women-folk scream their congratulations; is there a marriage, the whole neighbourhood is aroused by the clamour; is there a death, the whole neighbourhood is made dismal with heartrending wails of despair. The Scriptural requirement, " Rejoice with them that do rejoice, and weep with them that weep," is not so much quoted as enforced in China. The Chinese hurl their joys at one another, and deluge one another with their woes. And should a neighbour be writhing under some real or fancied wrong, what "tongue-batteries" are brought into requisition for the bombardment of a whole district!

Two facts, small in themselves but illustrative of much, are, first, that the whole family at meals dip their chop-sticks or gravy-spoons into the common bowls of fish or eggs or vegetables; and, second, that the main room of a dwelling-house is open to all comers from the threshing-floor of the village or the street of the town. It is regarded as a sort of annex to threshing-floor or street. In a word, except at night, it is practically the common property of the neighbourhood.

To Western folk, especially to insular English folk, whose closed street-doors are symbols of respectability in which there is a considerable percentage of aloofness, and whose houses are their castles, suggesting a survival of feudal barony, all this seems intrusive, abnormal, unbearable. But to the Chinese themselves it is a genial expression of a truth which was universally acknowledged in the good old days of yore —the brotherhood of man. And one or two of the dwelling-houses in any given district are pretty sure to have as an adornment of the "main door" a strip of red paper inscribed with hieroglyphs to the effect that "all below the skies are one family," the very sentiment which, in the West, embodied in the phrase "the federation of man," is regarded as an ideal goal of sociological progress. Only, with such large words as a motto, the Chinese, as we have seen, stop short at the clan or the neighbourhood, and exemplify their axiom in a very clannish and local manner.

In the country they often regard a man of another surname with suspicion, and in the towns a man from another part as an alien. A man from a distant province, whose dialect differs from their own, is regarded as practically a foreigner; and an actual foreigner, until he has become well known, as an " ocean fiend." * Like many a sentiment, then, that of universal brotherhood in China, however broad in theory, is exceedingly contracted in practice. But with such sentiments ingrained into the local consciousness, it but requires time, and intercourse with the rest of the country and the world at large, in order to worthily extend the scope of maxims which in themselves are limitless and universal.

* " Foreign devil " is literally " ocean fiend," and seems to be the Chinese way of spelling *pirate*. As applied to foreigners, it may be traced back to the sixteenth century, when, as Sir Rutherford Alcock relates, " Simon Andrade and Fernando Mendez Pinto sailed up the China coast with their fleet of thirty-seven vessels, plundering the tombs of seventeen kings of an ancient dynasty, in which treasure had been buried, making many piratical expeditions from Ningpo as a base of operations, and drawing down upon themselves the vengeance of the surrounding population, about 1545." (*Parliamentary Papers.*)

And here, perhaps, it is only fair to the Chinese to say that they have never claimed to be " Celestials " or subjects of a "Celestial Empire." This strange Western blunder will doubtless be as difficult to correct as any wild notion held by the Chinese about foreigners has proved to be. But the attempt should be made nevertheless.

Our mistake arose from a mistranslation on early diplomatic documents of the term " Celestial Court," a term applied to the Imperial palace to mark out the one " Celestial " in China—the Son of Heaven —in contradistinction from the millions of " Terrestrials " whom he governs. True, everything connected with him is more or less " Celestial." Being himself " Heaven's Son," his bodyguard are called " Heaven-soldiers," and his couriers " Heaven-messengers," but " Heavenly " always means *Imperial*, and the Empire itself is described in the phrase " (all) below the skies," or the Terrestrial Empire.

The assumption involved in the term is similar to that behind the old Roman phrase *orbis terrarum,* or " all the world." The Romans applied the term to their empire as comprising *all the world that was worth counting,* and the Chinese term has a precisely similar meaning. And nowadays, finding that there are Western nations counting, the Chinese, many of them, give the phrase its full breadth and use it of the mundane universe. Or, retaining its ancient significance as synonymous with *empire,* they have even asked, " How long did your Empress (Victoria) rule over ' all below the skies ' ? " Thus, whatever the term may mean, they are generally willing to share it with us, or even to apply it specially to a Western Empire such as the British. So that if we persist in translating " all below the skies " as " celestial " rather than " terrestrial," we must prepare to dub ourselves " Celestials " forthwith.

A low form of individualism with little or no organisation marks the savage. A low form of individualism with a degree more of social organisation
characterises the barbarian. The sacrifice of
individuality to an extended and comparatively
high social organisation results in a civilisation
like that of ancient Egypt, Assyria, India, and
China. There is a good deal of permanence, but
with it much stagnation.—*Josiah Strong, " The
New Era,"* p. 22.

CHAPTER IV

HUMANITY IN BUNDLES

CHINESE solidarity is chiefly clannish or
local, but within those limits is as patent
a fact as a rope-tied faggot or bundle of
firewood. In social intercourse within the
clan itself every effort is made to preserve
a secular edition of the unity of the spirit
in the bond of peace ; and a conciliatory
attitude is adopted toward every friendly
visitor who represents another clan or circle,
and who may perhaps bring the whole resources of that other bundle of humanity to
bear upon any real or imaginary affront.
There is always a lurking suspicion that
an outsider may be a possible foe at some
time or other. He is therefore treated

with a consideration which is half depre-
catory, and with a politeness that consists
largely in what may be termed the bribery
of flattery, which bribery he on his own
part returns with interest. Is his host
"humble" and his visitor "honourable,"
the visitor himself will describe himself
as "abject" and his host "opulent." But
the reason of it all is obvious from the
above considerations.

It is thus, surely, that the fine art of
Chinese guest-receiving has attained to its
present developments. It answers a similar
purpose to that of the buffer between
loosely-chained railway carriages, prevent-
ing a necessary contact from becoming an
unpleasant collision. Thus viewed, some
of its apparent absurdities will disappear
and many of its utilities will become readily
apparent.

By the long-enforced decrees of national
custom, the clan or locality is bound up in
a bundle that no efforts may divide, and

Confucius, as we have seen, did his utmost
to convert the whole Empire into a vast
clan-unit. The rulers of China have long
since agreed to regard it as such, and have
accepted the theory of personal responsibility for the whole empire-clan, representing national calamities as resultant from
Imperial sins against heaven. Thus on
an inundation of the Yellow River or the
occurrence of drought, the Son of Heaven
has proceeded to the Temple of Heaven and
made humble confession of personal delin-
quencies, which he afterwards confesses
also in an Imperial edict published in the
various prefectures and counties throughout
the Empire. But having set the example
in theory he enforces its observance in
practice, by recognising a very real clan-
responsibility as being shared by every
member of the multitudinous clan-circles
everywhere. "Each subject has not only
to consider his own individual responsibility
for his personal acts or lesions, but he

knows full well that his father, mother, grandparents, children, grandchildren, brothers, and sisters, down to the remotest links of the family chain, may have to suffer if he merits punishment." Nor is any rank of life in China exempted from the operation of this system of mutual responsibility. It runs in a regular gamut from the elder of the family to the head-man of the village, from the head-man to the local constable, from the constable to the inferior mandarin, and thence in regular succession to the county mandarin, the prefect, provincial Judge, Treasurer, Governor, and Viceroy. In some respects it is a terrible system, but the very reality of its awe-inspiring inevitabilities makes it an exceedingly useful system in the prevention of crime, or the capture of the criminal.

And on this latter point it may be added that the villainous-looking underlings of the mandarin we met in the streets of Shanghai are technically regarded, and not without reason, as, at any rate, " sleeping partners " in every local thief-gang. They themselves are held responsible for each robbery if the thief is not forthcoming, and, failing to arrest him, may themselves be put under arrest and punished with a fair amount of severity—always provided that their lord and master is really in earnest in putting the case through. For such things as " presents " are not entirely unknown in mandarindom.

Such is the Chinese system, then, and a very cleverly-devised one from the point of view of the government of Cathay. It was intended to fuse the Empire into one great whole, but the fusion has stopped short at the molecule. The result is comparable to a block of loose red sandstone rather than the intended granite—a sandstone block which has been considerably weather-worn by those national storms known as insurrections, rebellions, and revolutions, but which seems to retain its general shape nevertheless.

The Chinese instinct of solidarity is so forcibly absorbed by the system of local responsibility that it seems to have no overplus of energy toward a wider patriotism. Besides, China is so big, and its bigness is the more impressed on the Chinese mind owing to the crude native system of transport and locomotion. Our Western patriotism is not so contracted. An American finds his heart large enough to embrace the whole of the States, and, indeed, feeds his patriotism upon their very bigness. But each Chinese is a fraction of a unit inhabiting a continent, which he has been taught to regard as " all below the skies "; and what Englishman or European generally finds room in his bosom for stirring emotions which shall embrace the whole Continent of Europe?

The sole contingency which would tend to bring about that result would be some government, as that of the Manchu, arraying itself against the whole of Europe

—a state of things approximately brought about by the imperially-instigated enormities of 1900. And so, in China, while combination on behalf of one's own Empire seems too large an order to be executed, combination against a common foe, real or imagined, may be within the bounds of possibility, especially if that foe be represented to have dire intent upon the Chinese equivalents for hearths and homes and local interests everywhere ; if, in short, that foe be an invader.

Now, from of old the Chinese in country districts have been wont to regard every visitor from afar as an invader. And not without cause, for every autumn has witnessed the invasion of Mandarin So-and-So's grasp-all-you-can tax-collectors of evil visage. And it only requires a given amount of filthy slander (as in Hunan placards, *Death-blow to Corrupt Doctrines*, and such publications) to be freely circulated about the towns, and to be enlarged

upon in the village tea-shops, to bring about
a fairly universal cry of " Ocean fiend," and
to stir up inflammable emotions to ignition
point on special occasions. Thus doubly
have the Chinese authorities utilised existing instincts in the minds of a clannish
people; first, by the raids of their underling
extortioners, and secondly, by the assisted
diffusion of such atrocious slanders as
charges of eye-scooping for the concoction
of medicine, and the alleged practice of
customs too bestial to be described in
English type—but for which the " sacred
characters of the Holy Sage " have been
so freely brought into requisition. Thus,
through the reiterated efforts of a decade
have " patriotic " rioters been manufactured
from the riff-raff, and crimes against the
more unoffending harbingers of civilisation
committed either by the professed disciples
of Confucius, high in office, or by a
maddened populace whom they, during the
space of ten years, systematically and

designedly goaded on to madness. And thus it comes that a native Shanghai editor, who owes his very existence to the ægis of foreign protection (for all native newspapers were drastically "suppressed" by "Imperial Edict," October 8, 1898), calmly states in a leader of August 17, 1900, that "Ever since China established treaties of commerce (with the West), there is not a man claiming to be truly and bravely patriotic who has spent a single day without longing to get hold of the foreigner's flesh and eat it"—in savage satisfaction and cannibal revenge! But if this last item be fact, had we not better pause and sound an alarm?

Behold, ye nations of the earth, and tremble as ye gaze! Chinese Patriotism has awakened from an age-long sleep, and stands with hungry eye, lighting the fires of a cannibal oven, prepared for your reception. For the cupboard is bare, and the giant has nothing else to feed himself

upon but your shrinking flesh. And know,
O ye peoples, that not fairy-tales but
prophecies were the stories with which ye
amused your early days of innocency.

> " Fe fi fo fum ;
>   I smell the blood of an Englishman ! "

The giant's cry is no fiction, but became
literal fact in the closing months of the
nineteenth century anno domini !

A leading novelist makes one of his
characters say, " A foreign land will make
old bones of a man without the aid of
years," but amid the untold horrors of 1900
here was an element which made us feel
young once more. We were children again
by the old fireside, asking, " Mother, is that
all true ? Was the giant real? And did
he really and truly talk like that ? " Thus
did an extravagant sentence in Chinese
type awaken memories of an old home,
which home, in its turn, aroused emotions

in connection with the home-land—emotions which we recognise by the word *patriotic*.

The question remains as to whether the Chinese may not by any process of education become patriotic in the sense that we claim to be. A partial answer is given by I. T. Headland, who says, "It is one characteristic of the young reformers of China that they develop a patriotism which is akin to that of the West." Accepting that as a fact, let us ask whence young China learnt its reform principles and attendant patriotism. Surely from the West. And so the whole answer to our question is just this: "The Chinese may in time adopt true patriotic sentiments, but such *Chinese patriotism must be imported from abroad.*"

To us the life (of the Middle Ages) seems dull, and we can hardly realise getting through the wet days. . . . But it had the great advantage of making the men who were born to it accept existence with the acquiescence of a sluggish philosophy. It made them welcome, as excitements they might almost be grateful for, what we are in the habit of regarding as the "horrors" of those times.—*Blackwood's Magazine*, 1879.

CHAPTER V

THE process of huddling together is, in the long run, inimical to individual development, though it may be a necessary condition during certain incipient stages—which apothegm may be illustrated by reference to the common practice of rice-cultivation in China.

First of all the seed is sown closely together in a little plot, and soon grows up into a miniature field of dazzling emerald. But were it to remain thus, there would be little individual development among the rice-plants, and therefore a very small sum-total of grain from the whole. If China has become a notable example of

arrested development, it has been largely
due to the mechanical or social huddling
together of the populace inhabiting her
riverine neighbourhoods. There are too
many to the square mile literally, and the
crowds of individuals are much too closely
connected socially. They need planting out.

Once, in days of yore, China much re-
sembled ancient Greece in all but serrated
coastline. Her fourteen larger states, based
upon so many original tribes, were separated
by rivers and mountains, and developed
under the conditions of vigorous rivalry.
It was then that China produced her sages,
her classics, and her individuals. This was
in the period B.C. 1122–221, since which
she became a nation, but soon ceased to
be a nation of individuals. From that time
China, as a whole, has ceased to create,
and has devoted her energies to the fine art
of imitation. In religious matters she has
evolved her Taoism by this method.
Taoism is professedly based on the philo-

sophic musings of the Emerson of ancient China, Lao-tzŭ, the Venerable Philosopher, but in its later form is really a native modification of the Buddhism imported at various times during the earlier centuries A.D. In literary matters she has expended her energies in polishing and smoothing down existing attainments. And as to the populace, innocent of ideals religious or literary, we are reminded of a small boy with a copy well-written at the top of the page, who first copies it, and then copies his own writing line after line to the bottom of the page. A like phenomenon has been manifested in China on a big scale, and with a like result.

With us the prayer " Remember not the offences of our forefathers " is an expression of much that concerns our national life from Monday to Saturday, from January to December, and from generation to generation. It is the progressive instinct embodied in a petition.

The words are not a prayer for ancestors, as many Chinese familiar with the translated Book of Common Prayer somewhat naturally construe them. They indicate, on the one hand, a recognition of that family solidarity now covered by the word *heredity*; but, on the other hand, are the outcome of a desire to improve on the generations of the past—a desire which is diametrically opposed to all that is involved in the ancestral worship of China. The Chinese literally worship the preceding generation, and own themselves its inferiors—with a tendency to become such. And thus is ancestral worship, which drew forth such a solemnly eloquent paragraph from Carlyle, and which, as he says, should make audible the pulsings of the worshipper's soul, if he have any soul—thus is ancestral worship the very death-knell of progress. And even if, as some have argued, it were indeed harmless from a religious point of view, its down-dragging tendency is manifestly such as to call for its super-

session from national considerations. No
nation where it is generally practised can
be in anything but a down-grade condition.

To the learned, ancestral worship not only
involves reverence for the nearer progenitors
of the worshipper, but for the dead past of
custom and social condition under which
remoter ancestors lived ; and to the common people it means a disclaimer of any
effort to rise superior to " the offences of
our forefathers." And thus is produced a
social and national dead-level of malarious
bog-land, where, as evening shades close
around, the will-o'-the-wisp fires dangle
and dance. Originality is found, not in
character and achievement which may rise
above the ordinary, but in the superstitions
which haunt and flash above the general
bog.

It is amid such dead-levels that the life
of China's millions is lived out year by
year, until submission to the inevitable
has assumed the proportions of a national

characteristic. With no such hope as that "Whatever is is best," the man's whole environment has become identified with Fate, and the Chinese have become fatalists with a surrender to circumstances which may well surprise a resident from the West.

A Confucian scholar, engaged as pundit to an Englishman, had a remarkably clever son who had taken his literary degree in his early teens. And the proud father felt, what he would not admit in so many words, that his son would by and by develop into a still more distinguished personage than himself, and would "glorify the ancestral branch" even more than he professed to have done. Already had the youth exceeded his father's fondest hopes, and the outlook was in every way an ideal one.

But in process of time the young man fell ill. His complaint was readily curable by Western methods, and there was a skilled Western doctor at hand, whose services could have been secured for the asking.

After a considerable delay, and with due apologies to his ancestors who had used no such means, the doctor was called in, and prescribed two kinds of medicine which were to be taken at intervals. As a compromise with his ancestors the father administered but one kind, which happened to be the less potent of the two, and for want of the second the patient died. Next morning the father came as usual to give his lesson, and announced his bereavement by saying that the decrees of Fate were inexorable, and that the virtuous man ever submitted to them without a murmur. Otherwise the loss was as keenly felt as it would have been among ourselves. For a month later, when the pundit was asked to copy out a text of Scripture he had never seen before, the words " gave his only begotten Son " were blotted with falling tears. The Confucian Stoic was a human being still.

We have reason to suspect that much of the stoical bearing of the more highly

6

trained is assumed with the silken jacket in which the gentry pay their morning calls, and thrown off with that jacket on their return home. For in general matters the literati are sensitive to an extreme; and their efforts to " consume their own smoke," as Tyndall would have put it, can only increase that habitual sensitiveness. All such theories as seem to lift them above the passions common to humanity are, as has been hinted, worn outside the personality itself.

Nor is it in human nature to submit for long together with full acquiescence in such restrictions in general matters as those which form the subject of this chapter. The caged lark, however well domesticated it may seem to be, flutters against the bars now and then. The study of ancient literature, with its possibilities of material rewards to the few who excel, is itself an attempt to soar beyond the dead-levels of life. And the common people seek to escape the monotony of life in various ways.

A phrase which we can best translate as "noisy excitement" embodies one of the cherished ideals of the populace. And Buddhism had to assume a highly coloured form before it found acceptation to any general extent among the masses of China. And nowadays the Chinese seem quite unaware that the system of *Shih-chia-mou-ni* (Sakyamuni) ever contained such a dreary condition as that of Nirvana. So far as Nirvana can be regarded as a state to be enjoyed after death (rather than a condition of present possibility — and it seems to have meant both) it has long been replaced by the Western Paradise. And those few who have heard of *Ni-pan* (Nirvana) at all imagine it to be the name of a place in India.

Nor is Buddha himself the object of much worship. That has long been transferred to *Kuan-yin*, the Virgin goddess who brings sons to her suppliants among the women of China. Both of which innovations, as could be shown at length, being largely helped into being by early Nestorian teachings concerning the Christian heaven and the Mother of the Christ, when Nestorian missionaries from the West and Buddhist refugees from northern India met and fraternised in Tibet, previous to their Chinese campaign of the seventh century A.D., and following a general decadence of orthodox Buddhism in China.

So far from Chinese Buddhism finding its goal in Nirvana, the worship of Kuan-yin on the part of the sonless women of China has for its outlook a hoped-for escape from the Nirvana of nonentity, for a young bride is almost a nonentity until she has fulfilled the one acknowledged purpose of existence and has borne a son. That event alone raises her to the rank of an individual.

Then as to the Chinese love of excitement generally : a rude theatrical stage is erected in some country place, and over distances incredible and narrow field-banks innumerable, troops of tiny-footed women and girls converge in little processions toward the crowded hillock. And even such a small event as that of a relative arriving from a village a few miles away is often greeted by such excitement that the uninitiated might imagine a riot to be taking place. With the inflammability of long-dried faggots the Chinese populace catch fire on all possible occasions.

When festive events are scarce and life unendurably stagnant, a pot of the crudest samshoo may be brought into requisition. And the wonder is that the percentage of opium-smokers everywhere is not still larger than observation proves it to be.

The lad who has the making of a scholar in him is likely to be of finer grain than the rest, and to possess more latent capacities for realising the monotony of existence. And for such instincts Confucian study seems to provide an outlet, though that outlet is often more apparent than real. For years of drudgery are necessary before the hieroglyphics of yore are even known by name. Then follows the task of memorising the entire contents of every book which he studies. And only when boyhood is all but gone is there any initiation into the meaning of the whole. Nor is the task ended at this stage. It has only begun. For the outlook of classical study is to have at one's fingers' ends an antique style modelled upon that of twenty centuries ago, in a language which the ancients never spoke, and which would never have been understood by the disciples of Confucius had the Master conversed in such terse sentences. Imagine the New Testament and English History to be only procurable in a style like that of Latin telegrams, with a Latin commentary here and there, and you will gain some idea of the literature of China, apart from the forbidding hieroglyphics.

Yet in the hands of a ready writer this apparently impossible dialect has capacities of a style which shall be at once harmonious, delicate, and strenuous. In Chinese phraseology, the ideal essay possesses the complementary elements of " flowers and fire."

From the days when the Empire became such under the masterful and unscrupulous prowess of an ancient Napoleon of the Far East, some of the archaic ultra-tersities of the classics and historical books disappear, and a band of brilliant essayists enrich the national library to such purpose that the Western student ceases to wonder that Chinese pride finds its chief justification in the literary style of its tissue-paper tomes.

As on the walls of our own National Gallery, so on the walls of the Chinese Hall of Literature are inscribed the words : " The works of those who have stood the test of ages have a claim to that respect and veneration to which no modern can

pretend." And so the Chinese National
Gallery of Literature is daily crowded with
copyists who may venture to hope, amid
much despondency, to compose and treat
old themes for themselves by and by in
such a manner as to gain that highest
award of complimentary phraseology, "a
disciple of antiquity."

Among the crowd of ignorant and un-
learned country-folk, the Confucian scholar,
whatever his attainments, must necessarily
shine forth a genius of almost superhuman
calibre. For is he not a man of nightly
converse with the ghostly Sages who forces
them to yield up their sublime secrets ?
And should his scholarship be solid and the
fates propitious, he may tower above the
townsmen, too, as a qualified graduate
and mandarin, with rulership over five or
ten cities as his hardly-earned reward.

Contrasted with the masses, then, he
becomes a Gulliver among the Lilliputians ;
but contrasted with the ancients in his

mental outlook, he is as Gulliver among
the Brobdingnags. He has escaped one
dead-level to fall immeasurably below
another.

Its immense error lies in the assumption that what was once true is true for ever; and that a relation of ruler and ruled which was possible and good at one time is possible and good for all time.—*Herbert Spencer, "Study of Sociology,"* p. 36.

Be not the first by whom the new is tried,
Nor yet the last to cast the old aside.

Pope on " Criticism," line 335.

CHAPTER VI

IN our initial visit to Shanghai we saw
a countryman staring at foreign sights and
inventions, and a Chinese urchin smoking
a foreign cigarette, and may now proceed
to study them as types of two classes, the
one somewhat mystified by foreign ways,
and the other manifestly " emancipated "
and imitative.

If we follow the advice of the Leviathan
of Letters, and

> " Let observation, with extensive view,
> Survey mankind from China to Peru,"

we shall probably be struck with the fact
that humanity is readily divisible into two

classes : first, those in a rut, and, second, those not in a rut ; and feel also that the first class is further divisible into two subclasses : those who wish to be pulled out of the rut, and those who desire no such thing.

The countryman gazing at yon liberal allowance of telegraph and telephone wires is awaking to the fact that he has lived his life stuck in a rut—a respectable rut doubtless, by reason of the multitudes stuck therein, but a rut nevertheless.

Now he is a simple countryman, and ready to acknowledge with his lips what is passing in his mind. And having wondered awhile whether it is orthodox in a foreign street to cry " Excellent ! " or safe, with that Sikh policeman so near, to cry " Ocean fiend ! " he splits the difference by uttering the monosyllable " Ch'iao ! " which translates into our trisyllable " Marvellous ! " And thus saying, he confesses that he and his have been in a rut for ages.

Not so some smarter men. A native
who first saw a steamer at the mouth of
the Canton river years ago, refused to
express the astonishment he felt, and
calmly remarked, " My got plenty more
all same inside "—in the interior, that is,
before Chinese waters were opened up to
Western trade. And that sturdy Hunanese,
Admiral P'eng Yü-lin, whose prowess in
Mid-China battles with the Taipings brought
him to the front, gives us in his work
China's Indulgence toward Foreigners quite
an elaborate dissertation on the unorig-
inality of foreign inventions, in which
utterances the (unconscious) humour is
almost as delicate as in that sublime
fiction of Charles Lamb, *A Dissertation
on Roast Pig.*

He says : " Our philosopher Mo - stŭ
[fourth and fifth centuries B.C.], who discusses transmutations, is the founder of
Chemistry. What our ancient books say
of hairs and strings, their weight, &c., is

the beginning of the science of Mechanics.
What they say about two lights meeting
and forming an image on a mirror is the
beginning of the science of Optics. Our
philosopher Kang Tsang-tzŭ says water is
the refuse of the earth; vapour is the refuse
of water, and therefore is the founder of the
science of Steam. Our classic, the I King,
says there is a divine force in the earth,
and that when wind and thunder arise the
'dew' falls; this is the science of Electricity. Moreover, our Kuan Yin-tzŭ says
that fire arises from striking one stone
against another; that thunder and lightning arise from gases which can be made
artificially. Our Huai Nan-tzŭ [died B.C.
122] says that yellow earth, blue crystal,
red cinnabar, white jade, and black stone,
every year produce quicksilver. What is
above the fountain of the earth is cloud,
what results from intercourse of the *yin*
and *yang* principles is thunder; their clash-
ing produces lightning. Heat earth and

we get wood, heat wood and we get fire, heat fire and we get clouds, heat clouds and we get water, heat the water and we get earth again. Thus we in China discuss electricity very minutely. Now, these intelligent Western scholars took this teaching and developed it, and own that they cannot surpass what is recorded in Chinese books. But Chinese scholars, unacquainted with their own philosophers of yore, are foolish enough, when they see some strange thing used by foreigners, *to think of it as new !* "

And further on : " Do not think that the foreigner is truly skilled ; it is the Chinese who most excels in these skilful things after all " — the skilful things specially referred to being torpedoes, telephones, machinery, and locomotives — " only that *he does not care for them.*" Which utterance can only be excelled by a Chinese at Tientsin, some years ago, who, pointing to the telegraph wires, said to a missionary, "Have you got these Chinese things in your country?"

The man in a rut who does not want to be pulled out of his rut, gives as an all-sufficient reason that he was never in a rut at all. It needs some percentage of knowledge to reveal one's own ignorance.

Reading between the lines of that sturdy statesman just quoted, we may see, however, that it is the word "Foreigner" which is the crux of the whole difficulty. P'eng Yü-lin was an undoubted patriot, and there are many in China of all ranks and grades who, though not patriots, yet have sufficient national feeling to say, "Let us be pulled out of our rut by all means, but not by the foreigner." For on a return from any foreign treaty port they quote the foreigner as a somewhat masterful personage, as one who, added to his mastery of the applied sciences and arts, seems to claim a certain amount of mastery over men—"else how did he get his treaty port, and how has he retained it? Did not the illustrious founder of the Ming dynasty and builder of Nanking say, 'It is the birthright of the Chinese to govern foreign peoples, and not for these latter to rule in China'? And in his treaty port the foreigner manifestly rules, and feels it *his* birthright to do so." And this difference of opinion, natural on both sides, is the cause of much suppressed heart-burning — suppressed until opportunity comes for utterance, an utterance which may be somewhat explosive at times.

Even an enlightened official like H. E. Chang Chih-tung (Viceroy of Hupeh and Hunan), who has introduced ironworks, arsenal, cotton and silk mills, who employs foreigners and is in no sense their servant, has had to bear much popular obloquy, and has been nicknamed " Foreigners' Slave " even by neighbours and relatives of thousands who gain lucrative employment at

7

these "foreign" works. For there is ever the lurking suspicion that where foreign inventions are the order of the day, the foreigner's rule is not far behind.

Others see the advantage of foreign inventions, but feel that either the foreigner's religion, or his want of it, are inseparably connected with the adoption of such inventions. As to the foreigner's religion, the missionaries are proclaiming it everywhere; and as to his want of religion, a native paper of Shanghai says (July 18, 1900): "Foreigners who come to China completely lose the religion and restraints they received in their own lands. They walk disorderly without compunction, and ridicule everything"—words which are given as one argument out of many why " China cannot be Egyptianised."

There remains a class of Chinese to whom the word "Western" has undoubted attractions. They quote antiquity in support of their predilection for things from

the West. "West" from of old has been
a word to conjure with. The character
itself is an auspicious one. Its prominence
among Chinese characters, and its occurrence in certain combinations, point to
that region as the early home of the race.
Confucius is reported to have prophesied
the advent of a Sage in the West. Buddhism was accepted largely owing to the
fact that it came from the West. And
everywhere where the missionary has penetrated the fame of Western medicine is
great among the populace. So much so,
indeed, that a charlatan who puts up a
signboard labelled " Chinese and Western
Physician," even though, as in one case,
he be a runaway water - carrier with a
broken injection needle as his sole stock
in trade, will succeed for a while in commanding respect and in earning a living.

Then, certain advantages of foreign
citizenship are duly recognised, as, for instance, that foreigners do not have to kneel

in their courts of law, neither are they as witnesses subject to torture. And so, a few years ago, some clever swindler announced that he had foreign "B.A." buttons (!) for sale at a low figure, which would secure for their purchasers the above - mentioned privileges. And his dupes were many.

There are popular indications, then, that many would like to be pulled out of their rut, yes, and adopt foreign ways, if there were no foreign control mixed up in the matter. Was not the Emperor Kuang Hsü an illustrious instance of this before the *coup d'état* of 1898 ?

" The desire for foreign goods, toys, and inventions very early reached the child Kuang Hsü, and became a passion with him. . . . Phonographs, telephones, gramophones, graphophones, &c., were purchased for him, presented to him, or bought by him. . . . Then, later, he took up the study of the English language . . . purchased copies of both Old and New Testaments and all kinds of foreign books which had been translated into Chinese (eighty-seven, indeed, of the publications of the Christian Literature Society for China). These books embraced such topics as international law, political economy, chemistry, physics, botany, astronomy, mathematics, medicine and kindred topics, together with all phases of Christianity now preached or taught in the Middle Kingdom." He even "borrowed" the medical books of the wife of the writer of the above quotation. And, under an enlightened rule, such liberal-minded investigation would soon become fashionable, as the summer months of 1898 proved, when Reform was in the air.

Then there is a class of Chinese who readily take the colour of any new surroundings. Their imitative instincts are highly developed. One of the best-known facts about the Chinese is that a tailor will copy a foreigner's coat, patches and all. And many of the Chinese in the treaty ports learn to clothe themselves in foreign ways, to put on a metaphorical coat copied from the foreigner, patches and all. Yet, as a thoughtful writer has observed, "Imitation is the first principle of progress." The races which are not imitative are fast dying out, while those which have learned to imitate more progressive races, have themselves learned progress—a progress which will not long remain at the imitative stage.

There is a kind of Natural Selection in religion; the creed which is best adapted to the mental world will invariably prevail; and the mental world is being gradually prepared for the reception of higher and higher forms of religious life.—*Winwood Reade, " The Martyrdom of Man."*

The spiritual freedom which Christ came to give consists in moral force, in self-control, in the enlargement of thought and affection, and in the unrestrained action of our best powers.—*Channing, Sermon on " Spiritual Freedom."*

CHAPTER VII

IN our walk along Shanghai Bund, we saw
a gentleman whom a new-comer might at
first sight mistake for a Chinese, but who
on closer inspection proved to be a foreigner
in native dress, hence known among the
Chinese as the " Native Foreigner." This
witty Chinese phrase he is disposed to take
as a compliment, indicating as it does his
disposition to meet the Chinese half-way,
and not to make Westerners of them,
though his aim is to see them Christianised.
He is of course a missionary.

All missionaries do not adopt the native
dress, but those who do not, yet clothe
themselves with those motives which the

native dress symbolises. And perhaps it is not saying too much to affirm that all missionaries to China have to make up their minds toward a loosening of certain links which bound them to the society of their countrymen. That they have to be geographically severed from home is a condition which they share in common with their other countrymen in the Far East, and goes without saying ; but that they will be the subjects of a certain amount of criticism from those fellow-countrymen of theirs, both at home and on the spot, is a certainty which they accept together with the rest of their lot in coming to China. The man before us is a fairly well criticised man.

Imagining our visit to Shanghai to have been in the late summer of 1900, when the various warships and gunboats were making the phenomenon of " Jack ashore " one of the commonest elements of the season, we may have overheard a bluejacket (albeit

in white) saying to his chum concerning
the personage in the long robe and pigtail,
" That's the fellow that's been kicking up
all this fuss. If it weren't for him we
shouldn't be here." A specimen statement,
which, like most missionary criticisms,
opens up a wide field of inquiry. And as
we are now of an inquiring turn of mind,
let us try and examine the missionary *de
novo*, carefully eliminating any special
pleading for or against the man and his
doings. And let us attack the subject in
the form of question and answer, utilising
in our answers a quotation or two from
writers who may strike us as being as free
from prejudice as is possible for *genus homo*,
species writer, to be. And, to be more
than fair to the other side, let us abstain
from citing texts of Scripture which the
missionary might quote as his supreme
justification.

The first question is : *Why need he be
here at all?* Let us put that question to

the man himself, under the limitations just laid down.

He replies, "Because I could not help it."

How is that?

"Because I felt within my life a Power which has changed that life,—a Power so great that I have no doubt that it is adequate to change any number of other lives anywhere, in time. And not only do I as an individual feel that Power, but England has felt it as a whole more or less."

And he refers us to a scrap of print in his pocket-book, which says that a certain learned divine, preaching before the University of Cambridge in 1575, remarks that "before the preaching of the Gospel in Britain, no church existed but the temple of an idol; no priesthood but that of paganism; no God but the sun, the moon, or some hideous image. To the savage rites of the Druidical worship succeeded the abominations of a degenerate Roman idolatry. In Scotland stood the temple of

Mars; in Cornwall, the temple of Mercury; at Bangor, the temple of Minerva; at Malden, the temple of Victoria; at Bath, the temple of Apollo; at Leicester, the temple of Janus; at York, where St. Peter's now stands, the temple of Bellona; in London, on the site of St. Paul's Cathedral, the temple of Diana; and at Westminster, where the abbey rears its venerable pile, a temple of Apollo."

He tells us, moreover, that our question, "Why need you go at all?" was doubtless put to St. Augustine and those who preceded him. And as to St. Patrick, we have it in his own words (*Confession*, §15), "Whence came to me . . . that I should leave country and parents, and many of the gifts which were offered to me with weeping and tears? It was not my grace, but God who conquered in me . . .; so that I came to the Irish peoples to preach the Gospel."

"And," adds the missionary, "to leave the Chinese where they are, would be to show a lack of appreciation for the forces which have rescued us from heathenism, and made the difference between Queen Victoria and the Empress Dowager. Until we are prepared to return to the worship of the sun on Sunday, the moon on Monday, Tiu on Tuesday, Woden, Thor, Friga, and the Roman Saturnus, it is natural that we should try and bring to others the benefits of a Christian civilisation which has made all the difference between us and the Chinese."

The missionary's explanation will probably be accepted, though perhaps with a slight reservation as regards his last phrase. He seems to ignore various racial characteristics. Some Western lands, moreover, have been marked by certain geographical conditions inviting men sea-wards, and thus tending to bring about interchange of thought among various nations. So that they could not utterly stagnate, even if they had wanted to do so.

To which the missionary replies that this too was providential, and gave to such nations as the British not only the heritage of the seas, but a mission to break in upon the stagnation of sleepy nations beyond the seas. And as to the supreme means of dealing with that stagnation, he bids us remember the triple cross upon our Union Jack, which should never become a mere pictorial delusion like that of the Japanese sun upon the yellow banner of China.

He also quotes Heinrich Heine as saying : " Why do the British gain foothold in so many lands ? They are demanding, they are founding the great kingdom of the spirit, the kingdom of religious emotions and the love of humanity, of purity, of true morality, which cannot be taught by dogmatic formulas, but by parable and example such as are contained in that beautiful, sacred, educational Book for young and old—the Bible."

But "east is east and west is west," and it does not necessarily follow that a Gospel which suits the West should also meet the precise needs of the Orient, does it?

There is a good-humoured twinkle in the missionary's eye as he listens to our logic. We have obviously forgotten a fact which he himself has had forced upon his memory by his dealings with the Chinese, namely, that the manners and customs of the Bible are Asiatic, that our Lord and His apostles were Asiatics, and that it was an after-thought, and regarded by some as an audacious one, that a certain apostle should set out to evangelise Europe with the same Asiatic Gospel. And the argument is that what has so acclimatised itself in the West, to the extent that its Oriental origin may be forgotten for fifty-one Sundays out of the fifty-two, may well be expected to be accepted by an Oriental nation after a reasonable "length of time, proper scope

and opportunities "—to use a phrase of
Bishop Butler's.

*But how does it fit in with Confucian
ethics ?*

And here the missionary is ready with a
reply. He tells us that while no Gospel
will fit in with the modern " Confucianism "
of conscienceless mandarindom, the points
of contact between the Christian Gospel
and the general system of Confucian ethics
are many; that the Moral Philosophy
taught in our theological colleges is practically Confucian, having for its broad basis
the fulfilment of the relations subsisting
between man and man—between " prince
and statesman, father and son, elder and
younger brother, husband and wife, friend
and companion," to quote the list as given
in the Confucian books.

He explains that Christianity supplies
the sky to the Confucian landscape, and
the motive-force to the Confucian me-
chanism ; that the Divine forces appro-

8

priated by penitent faith and constant
prayer furnish the necessary impulse and
working energy for the whole; providing
for the destruction of the bias toward the
bad, and the attainment of all things true
and noble.

He tells us that some sort of a Supreme
was once recognised in China, and that in
China's most ancient dictionary—which is
made up of quotations from still more
ancient authorities — this Supreme is
affirmed to be "the producer of all
things," and also in a classic already old
in the days of Confucius, "the alone
Imperial Supreme, Parent of the people."
So that the way is prepared for the pro-
clamation of the truth that the Supreme
is our Heavenly Father. And that when
once this truth is accepted by the Chinese,
he gains a leverage such as would hardly
be available in the West. For in both
ancient writings and modern conversation
among the Chinese, the two terms *filial*

duty and *brotherliness* are most prominent ideals and the *sine quâ non* of all things admirable in character and conduct. So that these two terms, so deeply engraven on the Chinese conscience, have only to be lifted (on the one hand) to include the obligations to a Heavenly as well as an earthly parent, and broadened (on the other) into a benevolent interest in the welfare of brother-man, in order that the two prominent elements in the Christian system may flash out as peculiarly Chinese obligations. Thus viewed, Christianity furnishes the acknowledged supplement to the great duties proclaimed by Confucius, and, by means of its spiritual energy, not only makes such duties a possibility, but transforms the duty into a joy—as in the every-day life of many a Chinese convert.

With what success, then, has his Gospel been attended (say) in comparison with Buddhism and Taoism?

Let H. E. Chang Chih-tung (Viceroy of Hupeh and Hunan) reply. In a book published in 1898, for the perusal of the literati, he says, "The Western religion is daily flourishing; while the two cults (Buddhism and Taoism) are daily declining, and cannot last long. For Buddhism is on its last legs, and Taoism is discouraged because its demons are spiritless."

What methods has he used then?

Preaching, whether in halls or streets or country places.; Healing, whether in well-furnished hospitals or local dispensaries; Education, whether in colleges or elementary schools; Literature, whether on national subjects for the eyes of the literati, or Scripture translations and Christian booklets generally in language adapted to the populace at large.

He has dealt, then, with broad national questions?

Yes, as Professor Henry Drummond says, " There are two ways in which men who offer their lives to their fellow-men may regard the world. The first view is that the world is lost and must be saved; the second, that the world is sunken and must be raised." He sympathises with both views, but his immediate purpose being to represent the latter, he quotes China as " an instance of arrested development. On a fair way to become a higher vertebrate, it has stopped short at the crustacean. . . . The Christianising of such a nation as China is an intricate, ethical, philosophical and social as well as a Christian problem." And so among Chinese missionaries, there are, in his words, " a few Rabbis who will quietly reconnoitre the whole situation, and shape the teaching of the country along well-considered lines. . . . Such is the direct policy of many missionaries, and even of whole societies." Then, urging the need for more of this class, he says, " The missionary who has some philosophical training, who knows something of sociology and political economy, and who will apply these in Christian forms to China, is (in addition to existing workers) the man most needed at the present hour. For it is to be remembered that this is a case of arrested motion, and that the most natural development, certainly the only permanent one, will be one which is a continuation of that already begun, rather than one entirely abnormal and foreign."

But; what you call sociological questions apart, *have not the missionaries entangled themselves far too much in political matters?* Li Hung-chang, for instance, is reported to have said that the raising of the Roman Catholic missionaries to the grade of officials is responsible for the Boxer outbreak.

As a fact, the Jesuits and the Protestant missionaries in China are two distinct classes, as indeed they are in the West, and would naturally be everywhere. And as they took different ground on the subject of "official status for missionaries," so they adopt different standpoints generally, though happily with little personal feeling on perhaps either side. For in China a man's sympathies must either broaden or shrivel up, and a healthy broadening of sympathy, a cosmopolitan view of things, which need involve no sacrifice of principle, seems to be prevalent.

The differing relations which the two orders of missionaries sustain toward their respective governments will be readily inferred from two utterances from those best qualified to speak on the subject.

M. Pichon, as a deputy, was a Radical and a strong anti-clerical; as a Minister in China he has been the best friend of the clericals, declaring that "our missionaries in China are the best workers for the influence of France" (*North China Herald*, 13th October, 1900). Whereas Lord Salisbury, in his classical utterance on Protestant missions, says: "Missionaries are not popular at the Foreign Office." And the Chinese everywhere are shrewd enough to have found out that the relation of Jesuit or other Father in China is much nearer than that of any Protestant missionary to the government of his native land.

And now for a burning question of the day, and of many a day to come: *What share had the missionary in the great upset of 1900?*

The answer in brief is that he is both a reformer and a foreigner, and obnoxious to the ruling Manchu clique on both these counts. This reply will be the clearer on consideration of a brief statement of the inner history of the tragedy of 1900, which cannot be considered a national movement so much as a plot of the ruling Manchu, the young Emperor excepted.

China is an ambiguous term which includes three distinct elements: (1) the Manchu Government; (2) the Mandarins; (3) the Chinese populace.

(1) The Manchu Government is foreign,

and universally recognised by the Chinese
as such.   This is illustrated by a prohibited
book, widely circulated in manuscript, entitled *Push Him Out!* The basis of the
work is a series of picture prophecies pro-
fessing to date from A.D. 643, which are
interpreted with modern applications.   And
one of these pictures, in modern editions of
the work, represents a Chinese lad (young
China) pushing out a Manchu warrior.   The
situation would be paralleled if we could
imagine Russia to be ruled by Finland.

This foreign Government is jealous of
both Native Reform and of Western influence generally—in all of which it sees its
own existence menaced.   Its leading spirit
has been the Empress Dowager, an adven-
turess of genius, who, in September, 1898,
set aside the young Emperor, killed many of
his friends the Chinese Reformers, and then,
on November 5th of the same year, issued an
edict for the formation of Volunteer Corps
(as the "Boxers" have always been officially

termed) in all parts of the Empire, "to turn the whole realm into an armed camp in case of need." This edict was only taken seriously in the northern provinces, among existing Volunteer Leagues (described at length by a writer in *The Chinese Recorder* some years before). They were anti-Manchu, but were bought over and vigorously fostered by Manchu officials in high places, who had been substituted for Chinese mandarins for that very purpose.

These preparations having been effected, an edict was issued, June 17, 1900, ordering the destruction of all foreign property by fire, and the extermination of all Western foreigners and their Christian adherents by torture. This had been suggested by a Manchu adventurer named Yung Lu, in writing, early in the year. Two Chinese patriots at Court, since executed as traitors by being sawn asunder at the waist, made bold to reverse certain words of the edict to "strenuously protect," before sending copies to the centre and south of China. But the copies for the north passed through unaltered in spite of them. Where atrocities have occurred, they have been perpetrated in direct obedience to these unaltered edicts.

(2) The Mandarins, or magistrates. These are mostly Chinese, and for the greater part have acted for their own safety from Western retribution, and thus for the peace of China, and (helped by the reversed edicts) have neglected to take up the scheme of the Manchu-foreigner for the extermination of the Western foreigner.

(3) The Chinese populace, caring little for politics, and desiring to feed and breed in peace, but containing rowdies and vagabonds in every large centre—an element which the Manchu Government, through the mandarins and their underlings, has every now and then succeeded in stirring to violence, ever since the Tientsin massacre of 1870.

So strong has been the influence of the

Manchu Court indeed, as proved by the various anti-foreign edicts which have come to light, that one marvels at the comparative uninflammability of the populace, in not having enacted more tragedies than have already taken place. And one can only guess how few those uprisings against the available foreigner (the missionary far away from gunboat protection) would have been apart from such pressure from high authority.

But let us content ourselves with the easily proven answer to our question :—The missionaries have had a share in bringing about the upset of 1900, for the reason that they could not but be obnoxious to a Manchu clique which stopped not short at the murder of some of the finest men of light and leading among the Chinese, and would even depose a Manchu Emperor when he had thrown in his lot with the native reformer and with the missionary from afar—as much of the unpublished history of 1898 proves him to have done.

In the German Renaissance designs of the sixteenth
century, a not infrequent design is Aristotle
ridden by Phillis, whip in hand. And quite
commonly in Nuremburg work, a long-bearded
man appears ridden by a young woman.—*Art
Workmanship*, vol. i. part 2.

Eating deadly poison, so as to poison the tiger (whose
jaws are feared).—*Chinese Proverb*.

CHAPTER VIII

THE condensed statement of the causes of the upset of 1900 with which the previous chapter ended, would seem to invite expansion, especially as the whole series of facts forms a drama as thrilling as any that have been acted during recent centuries upon the great stage whereon all are actors.

The first scene opens with the introduction of a Manchu girl (born 1835), as imperial attendant into the dissolute Court of the throned debauchee, Hsien Fêng, somewhere in the fifties. The half deified weakling who became her master—but whom she was to dominate in the end—

is described by contemporary writers as "tottering to his grave, a decrepit, worn-out man of barely thirty years of age" in 1861. Yet did not his life stand out in glaring contrast to his environment, for it is generally understood that he had a Court to match.

During the year of his enthronement began the Taiping rebellion, and his death did not see the end of it; although in 1855, nine years before its close, this same weak monarch, feeling that the situation was getting desperate, issued an edict declaring that a certain hero of the third century, and one who had been half deified in 1594, had appeared in visible form, had crushed the Taipings, and was therefore to be worshipped as a god indeed throughout the length and breadth of the land. And thus it came to pass China lavished fresh epithets upon her pseudo saviour, applying to him the term most used by Christians of all kinds for the Holy Spirit. Neither

was all this in contrast to the times, for
the alleged successes of China's "god of
war" with the Taipings were on a par with
those of his patron, the Son of Heaven, in
governing the Empire.

Measuring her man, the wily slave-girl
wormed herself into his good graces, and
became the mother of a son whom he
nominated as his heir.

Meanwhile, the insolence and treachery
of a certain Imperial Commissioner named
Yeh provoked a fresh Western war with
China, and in 1860 the combined forces
of England and France were thundering
at the gates of Peking. The Emperor
Hsien Fêng fled with his wives and slaves
to Jehol in Manchuria, and utterly refused
to treat with the "outer barbarians." But
a brother of his, one Prince Kung, came to
the front, and conducted negotiations with
considerable ability and success.

The Emperor died in exile during the
next year (1861), and eight Regents were

appointed during the minority of the son of
the slave-girl.   But intrigue and jealousy
were rife.   They were killed, and the
mother of the child made Regent in their
place.   And it soon became a proverb at
Court that it was no use resisting the
young upstart, for she invariably succeeded
in everything upon which she set her mind.
Her various critics were fain to hold their
peace of set purpose, or were constrained
to do so by such gentle persuasives as the
lictor's rod, the silken cord, or the heads-
man's axe.   And all the courtiers thought
her wise—wise with that particular kind of
wisdom in vogue at the Dragon Court.

In 1864, a certain Governor of Kiangsu
(the province in which Shanghai is situ-
ated), one Li Hung-chang, who had
" employed some foreigners " in connection
with the Taiping rebellion in those parts,
claimed the credit of General Gordon's
successes, and the Empress Dowager
reaped the benefits thereof.   It was her

position which the "ever invincible army" of the foreigner made secure.

The next event of note was the murder of the French Consul, one or two priests, and nearly a score of sisters of the Romish Foundling Home, Tientsin, which building was burnt by a mob (June 20, 1870).

Two accounts are given of the occurrence. A high Chinese statesman (P'eng Yü-lin) says, "In the reign of Hsien Fêng, the French sent missionaries to travel in all directions and to establish churches; then bad people, under pretext of believing the new doctrine, entered the Church to obtain protection, cheated the country people, tyrannised over the orphans and the weak, debauched men's wives, robbed men of their property; and even when found out, the French missionaries secretly protected them, hid them in their churches, or sent them abroad to foreign countries. The people became highly indignant, rose up *en masse*, bent on revenge, burnt the churches and beat the missionaries (at Nanking and Yangchou), and the Tientsin massacre followed. . . . All this is the fault of one Church—the Roman Catholics. France alone is bent on Missions. . . . The Franco-German war really began with their religion. Spain says that France has a bad reputation. She has brought it on herself; who else can she blame?"

For the Tientsin massacre, France and other nations blamed a certain ex-Taiping rebel, Ch'en Kuo-jui, then Imperial general. He was a favourite of Li Hung-chang and a hater of foreigners. And it happened that the lesser disturbances at Nanking and Yangchou, and the massacre at Tientsin, took place during his residence at the three places. Prince Kung excused him by saying, "It was by accident that the General Ch'en Kuo-jui was present at Tientsin. He was sick and on a voyage; he had nothing to do with what took place." But Ch'en boasted that he had very much

indeed to do with the occurrence. And at
length the Tsungli Yamên admitted that he
had used "some idle words" just about
the time it took place. Which amounts
to a full confession of his share in the
deed.

There was also another actor, one Chung
Hou ; his office, Foreign Negotiator (Tao-
t'ai, ranking next the Governor of the
province); his official salary, £100 per
annum ; his acknowledged income from
bribes and extortions, over £100,000 per
annum. And as the Ambassadors pressed
for his degradation, he was removed—to a
higher office elsewhere. Which has become
the custom after later riots.

When urged to say whether he thought
dismissal was a sufficient punishment for
those responsible for the lives of some
twenty foreigners, Li Hung-chang, who had
just been made Viceroy of the province, at
length admitted that they were worthy of
punishment, but *only because a foreign*

consul had been killed, not if the sufferers
had only been missionaries or traders.*

As a consul had been killed in this case,
what was the punishment meted out to the
General Ch'en Kuo-jui, who had boasted
that the deed was chiefly his own ? He
was received in audience by the Imperial
son of the Empress Dowager, and returned
to Tientsin as the friend of Li Hung-chang.

And immediately after, the fan-shops were
requisitioned to provide a novel form of
comfort for the ensuing summer—to manufacture thousands of fans whose device was
a foreign building in flames, foreigners
being killed, and a Chinese mandarin rising
from his chair and urging the people on to
take their part in the work of merit. (For
a reduced facsimile of one of these fans, see
The Graphic, November 26, 1870.) The

---

* This corresponds with what Li Hung-chang said
in August, 1900, of those imprisoned in the Legation
buildings in Peking :   " The   rest (besides the
Ambassadors) do not count—do not count at all."

sales were enormous, and a general massacre of foreigners throughout the Empire seemed imminent.

France was now entangled in the war with Germany; and as to the other Powers, "the system of trifling with foreign Ministers" was so successful, that only after a long time were these fans nominally suppressed.

The Empress Dowager thus learnt an important lesson, namely, that under certain circumstances, foreigners and even foreign officials might be murdered by an officially-stirred mob, and little besides verbal protests would result—a lesson which she treasured up in her heart. And why, after all, should foreigners have more immunity from death than eight Regents, and others whose slaughter was to follow?

In 1874 a party arose whose purpose was to break the power of the Empress Dowager whom they called an outsider, and to raise the son of Prince Kung to the throne.

Prince Kung being brother to the deceased Hsien Fêng, and a man of great ability, it was argued that his son had, at any rate, as good a claim to the throne as had the son of the ex-slave girl, especially as her son inherited many of the weaknesses, if not all the vices, of his father.

Li Hung-chang was now Viceroy at Tientsin, and to him the Empress Dowager appealed. He accordingly made a secret forced march on Peking with four thousand men, was admitted into the outer gates of the city at midnight, and then into the Forbidden City, as arranged. All the palace guards on duty were disposed of and replaced by Li's men. And in the morning, the friends of Prince Kung's son were surprised, disarmed, and sent away to death or exile. And again was the Empress Dowager mistress of the situation.

Her son, the nominal Emperor Tung Chih (United Rule), died on January 12, 1875; but his death was not announced till some time afterwards. Instead, nine days after he had died, the *Imperial Gazette* (Jan. 21) stated that in token of rejoicing at his convalescence, his Majesty conferred various dignities and donations and showed forth his Imperial clemency in many ways. And why, forsooth, should foreigners have more immunity from deception in China than the whole Chinese nation itself at this and other times ?

On March 27th the widow of Tung Chih died. The *Imperial Gazette* of that date accounts for her death by saying that "When called upon to lament the departure of His Majesty the late Emperor to be a guest on high, her grief was so excessive that it took the proportions of a fatal illness." But the facts were that the expectant mother happened to drink a cup of wine in which poison was mingled, and died in agony therefrom. And all China is persuaded that the Empress Dowager on that day murdered her own daughter-in-law and the child she feared that daughter-in-law would bear. And, again, is it within reason, that foreigners alone of all folks that stood in her way should be preserved alive?

The Empress Dowager now nominated her nephew, Tsai-t'ien (Kuang Hsü), a child of four, as puppet Emperor, whose strings she could pull at will.

The new chapter, which we may call Act III., opened by the treacherous murder of H.B.M. Consul Margary by Chinese troops on February 20, 1875, while in the province of Yunnan on an expedition which had been fully sanctioned by the Manchu Court. For months the Tsung-li-Yamen prevaricated and delayed, on the ground that they had received no official report of the murder. And although a mediator was appointed in the month of August, and the matter discussed in the Chefoo Convention of September 13th, no official settlement of the case took place till October, 1876.

And about this time were issued, under official patronage, several inflammatory works, three in particular accusing foreigners of such practices as eye-scooping for the purpose of obtaining eight pounds of silver from every hundred pounds of Chinese lead, explaining that "the eyes of foreigners are of no use for this purpose ; they must be Chinese eyes." Also that "every seventh day all Christian foreigners assemble in a church, and when the ceremonies are over give themselves up to debauchery," and many like words. And over a million copies of one of these works were circulated free.

Then later arose one Chou Han, in the Hunan province, whose pictorial descriptions of the "ocean fiends" and their atrocities were also circulated by the million. And as this same Chou Han was not in any remunerative office, the expenses had to come out of official funds.

And so, in 1891, various foreign property was destroyed at various places along the

Yangtse, and two foreigners—one not a missionary, and the other not known to be a missionary—were murdered in a riot, and the mandarins of the place did nothing to save them, but rather were the ringleaders of the riot none other than the mandarins' underlings.

And so Chou Han issued a new placard, representing these two foreigners as being exterminated by soldiers of the Government.

The young Emperor Kuang Hsü, having come of age, issued an edict of surprised remonstrance at these riots and murders. But the Empress Dowager sent to the various viceroys secret commands which made the edict null and void.   And so there were more riots and massacres during the years which followed.

And when these riots had taken place and foreigners had been killed, the Western press is said (by a Far Eastern secular paper) to have argued in the following strain :—

" Seizure of territory by foreign governments, forced railway and mining conces-
sions, disturbing ancestral tombs and
temples, opium importation under protest,
and other forced aggressions upon the
Chinaman, are things he rather likes. You
see, that is what he is there for, and so he
has long realised that his wealth and
resources are for the foreigner to exploit.
But missionaries are a continual menace
to the Empire. They come along and dis-
tribute themselves throughout the country,
say about one in two hundred thousand
natives, and begin to translate Bibles and
text-books, preach and proselyte, build
schools and hospitals with abominable
foreign money, teach foreign languages,
foreign science, foreign religion, and foreign
medicine. This is too much for the Chinaman, and so he rises up in his wrath, and,
of course, in his unreasoning madness, he
makes all foreigners suffer alike.

" If only the abominable missionary

could be driven out, and the other peaceable foreigners left to their railroads and mines, justice would be perfected."

And all this reasoning was very welcome to the Empress Dowager and her party, and might be of immense aid to her in case of any great move. For all would then say that the movement was only against the missionaries.

And now, as the drama was enacted in China, we may allow a new character to appear and describe himself as Chinese actors do. And this is his speech :—

"I am of about the same age as the Empress Dowager, and, like her, I am an adventurer. Seeing how she had risen, I too cherished the ambition to rise—ay, to rise above her in the end. My name is Yung Lu, and from a humble Manchu home I worked my way up in the graces of the Empress Dowager until she conferred upon me the three highest military offices in the capital. But I was proud, and bowed not to Li Hung-chang, and was insolent to others, until I lost office. Yet I soon began to rise once more, and am very retiring now, letting others hatch my plots and bear the brunt of them. And as the drama progresses, you will see how I can dethrone an Emperor, who knew I was aspiring to the throne, and how I can involve the Empress Dowager and my rivals in power, Prince Tuan and the rest, in sore disgrace with the foreigners. They will never suspect me—unless one of them who has friends in the palace gather all the facts and verify them."

An interesting actor this! Let us watch him; for all that he has prophesied may come true—even the last item.

In the year 1898 the young Emperor, whom the Empress Dowager had at last allowed to rule, surrounded himself with those who sought the welfare of the realm, who saw its needs, and determined to meet them. But as Yung Lu was proved to harbour treacherous designs, it became necessary for the Imperial safety to remove him. Averse as the young Emperor was to bloodshed, he entrusted a warrant for the execution of Yung Lu to the young patriot Tan Tze-tung, to deliver in secret to the general Yuan Shih-kai, who seemed faithful, but who was really a sycophant of Yung Lu just then. He betrayed his Emperor to Yung Lu, who betrayed him to the Empress Dowager. Then did the Empress Dowager upbraid the Emperor to his face and confine him to his rooms for some days; during which time all the Reform edicts were reversed and the Emperor's co-patriots killed. And as the patriot Tan Tze-tung went to execution he cried, "They may kill my body, but for each man killed there will be a thousand others in whom my spirit shall live." And those who heard the words treasured them up, and wondered whether the prophecy would ever come true.

Then the eunuchs and others who were favourable to the Emperor were beaten to death, for the custom of the Manchus forbids that any one should use swords within the palace itself. And the Emperor, being in danger of his life, appealed to the British Embassy to protect him. For he had one left who could deliver a message faithfully. And that messenger was repulsed and told to hold his peace. . . .

Just forty days after that fatal 26th of September (the date of the *coup d'état*) began a Gunpowder Plot which was to shake the world eventually, though none knew what it would mean in the end just then. On November 5, 1898, the Empress Dowager issued the edict ordering the formation of " Volunteer Corps " (otherwise translated " Righteous Harmony Leagues," which foreigners have called " Boxers ") " to turn the whole nation into an armed camp in case of need."

Also, within a few weeks of the *coup*

10

d'état, Tung Fu-hsiang boasted publicly that the object of the great military preparations which were then starting was "to drive all foreigners into the Yellow Sea."

Then, on November 21st, the Empress Dowager issued instructions to the Viceroys with regard to dealings with foreigners, and said, "Never should the word 'Peace' fall from the mouths of our high officials, nor should they even allow it to rest for a moment within their breasts."

In May and June, 1899, "the Lord High Extortioner," Kang Yi, started on his tour, carrying the Empress Dowager's renewed instructions ordering the Viceroys everywhere to form Volunteer ("Boxer") forces in their respective provinces, and collected about a million ounces of silver to aid the Boxers of the North. But though the Viceroys of the Yangtse could not but subscribe to the fund, they memorialised the Empress Dowager, protesting against the Court patronage of these same Northern Boxers.

Yü Hsien was now Governor of Shantung, and his under-officials were so oppressive that on July 13th "certain of the country people banded themselves together for defence." These are the facts, but in an edict which these facts called forth, their action is described as "brow-beating the authorities."

To the Empress Dowager's own "loyal Boxers" Yü Hsien distributed arms, and on December 27th proclaimed that "they might loot, plunder, burn (any foreign premises), but they must not take life." But on December 31st they went beyond their instructions, and took the life of Mr. S. M. Brooke. The British Government accordingly asked for the degradation of the Governor Yü Hsien, as both treaty clauses and passport regulations had been openly violated. He was "degraded" to a higher post. From Governor (the rank below a Viceroy) he was made Viceroy in Shansi. And on the way he was received by the Empress Dowager " with every mark of favour, for she gave him a breastplate on which she herself had embroidered the word ' Happiness.' " And his place in Shantung was filled by Yuan Shih-Kai, who had betrayed his Emperor to Yung Lu (September, 1898), as a reward of merit on that former occasion. And the Foreign Ambassadors saw these things, and protested not. And missionaries made representations, but they were unheeded by the Legations. For there was no place in China in which missionary criticism was so rife, as in these Legations, and " every one knew that the movement was a purely anti-missionary affair."

And now, as the final act of the drama opens, Yung Lu saw his chance. He saw that the Empress Dowager had exasperated those who loved their land, by issuing a decree (January 24, 1900), ignoring the

Emperor Kuang Hsü, and nominating (as the heir of her deceased son Tung Chih) a Manchu lad of nine years of age, who could neither write nor speak Chinese, namely Pu-chun, son of Prince Tuan—whereat, from Shanghai alone came a remonstrance from 1,231 Chinese citizens, also like remonstrances from other parts; and from Siam a memorial from 80,000 Chinese, threatening to come with armed force and fight the cause of their deposed Emperor; and like memorials from other places beyond seas. He saw that the Emperor Kuang Hsü, being denied the aid of England when his life was endangered in 1898, had lately written to the Emperor of Japan, calling him brother, and praying to be rescued. And that the Empress Dowager was mad with anger at such subjects, at the Emperor, and all men beyond the sea who favoured the Emperor. And so Yung Lu prepared his scheme for her overthrow and his own succession to the Dragon throne.

Direct audience was difficult to gain, especially in secret, for the young Emperor still had a few friends unslain at Court, and thus it came that Yung Lu's plot was put in writing (and that the plot was proved to have been his own). And this was the scheme thus propounded while yet the year was young, namely: taking advantage of the fact that the Ambassadors had quoted the Boxers as only anti-missionary, to surprise, imprison, and kill them every one, and then to have all foreigners throughout the Empire killed also. He urged that besides Her Majesty's "Tiger troops" there were the "Volunteers" whom Yü Hsien had armed, and were these "Volunteers" yet more encouraged, everything would be ready for the great undertaking by the ninth day of the ninth moon (October 31st). This was the ancient Feast of the Moon (when cakes were made to the Queen of Heaven, as in Jer. vii. 18), called in the Chinese the Festival of *Ch'ung-yang*,

Renewal of the Virile Principle of Nature, but now by a pun, " the expulsion of the foreigners."

Later on, however, it was concluded that the nation would not consent to such a deed upon a joyous festival, and so the fifteenth day of an inauspicious intercalary month (the eighth moon) was the day appointed, for the reason that on that day of ill omen the nerves of a superstitious nation would be at their weakest, and *all would be fearing some calamity.*

But so liberally were the " Volunteers " nourished from the national funds (as their receipted documents discovered at Tientsin attest), and so rampant did they grow under such nourishment, that they soon began to precipitate matters. So that the date of the general massacre would have to be altered for one much earlier. Which was deemed unfortunate, as all the preparations had not yet been completed. But Yung Lu sorrowed not. His plot against the Empress Dowager was working !

Anon the Ambassadors began to inquire drowsily whether everything was, after all, so purely anti - missionary as they had dreamed ; and on May 22nd remonstrated with the Tsungli Yamên, and threatened to bring military guards up to Peking. On May 31st those foreign guards started. There was no opposition, for the time of arousal was not meant to be yet. But the Boxers grew more and more rampant, killing a few foreigners. And the " great undertaking " must be inaugurated very soon if at all.

So on June 17th Prince Tuan put into shape the suggestion of Yung Lu, and drafted an edict for the Empress Dowager's approval, and it was worded thus :

" To the Viceroys and Governors of the provinces. . . . Whether foreign dwellings or doctrine-halls, all are to be consumed by fire ; whether foreign official or merchant, missionary or convert and the like, all are to be destroyed by torture. There is to be no pity shown, as that would spoil the great undertaking."

The Empress Dowager agreed, and, as in the Book of Esther, there was written unto all the lieutenants and to the governors that were over every province, according to the writing thereof : in the name of the Empress Dowager was it written, and sealed with her seal.   And the letters were sent to all the northern provinces, to destroy, to kill, and to cause to perish by torture, all foreigners and all believers of the foreign teaching, both young and old, little children and women, and to leave none alive.

And so, in these northern provinces, (say) three hundred foreigners who were missionaries besides many who were not called by that name, and (say) fifteen thousand native converts perished.   And the Ambassadors themselves were imprisoned for the space of two months, and one of their number was killed by the soldiers, and the rest were rescued with great difficulty by the bravery of many troops and the loss of many brave lives.

For, as a British statesman showed in the House of Commons (August 2nd) : " Since 1895, firms in this country had supplied the Chinese Government with 74 guns of position and 11,740 rounds of ammunition ; 123 field-guns and 40,000 rounds ; and 297 machine-guns with over 40,000,000 rounds. And Germany had supplied nearly half a million Mauser rifles with 3,000,000 rounds." But these figures, as he said, did not pretend to be exhaustive. And both countries had supplied military instructors, and instructors to build arsenals in which the Manchu Government of China might manufacture enormous quantities of large guns and Mauser rifles on the spot, ever since 1895, following the visit of Li Hung-chang to the West, who left England saying that the British were " a frank and simple people," words which in Chinese mean, "those of whom the wily may take advantage."

And now did the Empress Dowager flee to the westward, taking her Imperial nephew with her, and continued to urge the Viceroys and Governors at all costs to resist the foreigners. And on November 19, 1900, Li Hung-chang, having been appointed Peace Commissioner, sent a secret message to the Viceroys and Governors, written in his own name and worded : " Peace affairs hard to settle. Prepare war ! " And this same message was shown by one of the Viceroys to the Lord High Commissioner of the Yangtse, Pelham Warren, and to Admiral Seymour in the city of Wuchang (November 26th).

And, apart from the brave words and deeds of Tan Tze-tung in the capital before his execution, is there nothing in the whole drama for the audience to applaud—nothing besides the intrigues of a corrupt Oriental Court, among high-climbing adventurers who had dropped their consciences to climb aloft upon a pile of human corpses, and who would risk a nation's ruin to gain their own selfish ends? Verily there is; one scene remains, and we who look on and judge shall indeed be judged as heartless if it stirs no deep emotions within us.

The edict of extermination had gone to the northern provinces, but when a miscreant named Li Ping-hêng, who had been made Admiral of the Yangtse, returned to the capital towards the end of June—his path from the Grand Canal to the capital being marked by burnt Mission stations and the corpses of Chinese converts—his Mistress questioned him as to what the Yangtse viceroys were doing toward the great undertaking which she had commanded. And he told her that instead of exterminating the " ocean fiends " they were protecting them! Then she called for the two high statesmen to whom she had entrusted her edict of extermination, to know if they had indeed sent it to the centre and south of the land.

Now it had come to pass, earlier in the month, when these two high statesmen, Hsü Ching-chên and Yuan Ch'ang had received the edict to forward to the centre and south of China, that they saw its execution would entail untold calamities on the realm; and feeling that appeal on that point was useless—for they had been thrice repulsed before—they altered the words "consume by fire . . . destroy by torture" to "strenuously protect," and forwarded the altered edict to the centre and south provinces, where it was posted for all to see. Then, knowing that their lives were endangered, they sent away their wives and dependents from the capital, lest they too should suffer from the fury of the Empress Dowager.

But one faithful dependent of the statesman Yuan, his private secretary, who knew all about the altered edict, refused to leave his master, and arranged to remain in Peking at the house of a merchant who was trusty, so that he might receive letters and forward them, and watch as to what became of his master. And he was glad at heart, for nothing happened—until the return of Li Ping-hêng. . . .

The two statesmen being called into the inner palace, the Empress Dowager asked them to account for the state of things which the Admiral of the Yangtse had described.

Bowing to the ground, the two men said with tears, " Your ministers felt they must save both Court and populace, and secure the realm from calamity ; and for that reason dared to alter certain words in the decree. They know that their lives are forfeit for the offence, and only supplicate that their households may not suffer the death-penalty too. This they will deem an act of clemency indeed."

The Empress Dowager, with that wonderful command of countenance for which
she is famous, heard their confession
without moving a muscle. But Prince
Tuan and Li Ping-hêng reviled the two
statesmen in a loud voice, and knelt and
prayed that the two traitors be destroyed
from beneath the spreading heavens. Then
the Empress smiled that " cold smile," so
dreaded at Court, and commanded that
they be executed forthwith by being placed
in the instrument called the " rotary
barrel," which is reserved for those guilty
of high treason, and cut in sunder at the
waist.

And it was done.

Then, on the 28th of June, a fresh edict
was sent to the centre and south of
China, recounting the victories of the
" Volunteers co-operating with the Imperial
troops throughout the province of Chih-li;"
praising the bravery of " these loyal subjects," who were surely to be found every-

where throughout the Empire, calling upon all Viceroys and Governors to raise forces from their number, and requiring the Yangtse Viceroys " to use their most strenuous endeavours to put these instructions into effect." But they (having so lately received an edict to protect " foreign dwellings and doctrine-halls, missionaries, converts, foreign officials, and merchants ") quoted this second edict as coming from Prince Tuan, whom they considered as " a rebel. And decided not to obey these decrees from Peking." (See China Blue-book, No. 3, 1900, p. 93.)

Reader, have you any friends, men, women, or little children, left alive from the year 1900 in the realms of the Empress Dowager? If so, tell your own little ones, and weep perhaps as you tell them, how it comes to pass, under God, that those friends are yet alive. . . .

The severed bodies of the two heroes were gathered up lovingly by their friends

whom they had made at Court, and in
process of time sent to the native place of
the two men, near Hangchou, in the Chêh-
kiang province, among the most famous hill
and lake scenery of China.

And on the 4th of November the gentry
of Hangchou gathered to pay their last
respects to the two who had loved the
country which the others despised. Crowds
were present, and among them some
Western sympathisers. And the fact that
these two statesmen, and not the Court
intriguers, represent the nobler public
feeling of the nation, is embodied in the
elegy which was recited on that occasion.
This, being published in the native papers,
has gone into many provinces, and nowhere
without evoking keenest sympathy. Re-
produced in humble translation, the reader
will feel that the lines represent not so
much the skill of the Chinese elegist, as the
deep feeling of the human heart when con-
fronted by such nobility of character as

11

may well be celebrated throughout the wide world.

THE ELEGY.

So firm of purpose that we thought, alas,
"Two hearts in one could snap the bars of brass."
All undismayed at each successive ill,
Ye swore to save the Realm—ah, dauntless will!
The Realm whose steps were tott'ring as ye knew,
For not in book-lore versed alone, your view
Comprised the many perils of the State;
Ye saw the times were troublous, full of fate,
Yet made your venture, rowed against the tide—
That storm-swept torrent that ye had not tried.
Thrice, weeping tears of blood, ye prayed and
    warned,
"True words offend the ear," your words were
    scorned.
And so ye died, died leaving legacy
Of heart-ache sore, at martyred loyalty.
Sincere of soul, ye fell; the pit was deep;
Your feet were snared—and it is ours to weep.
Yet, far beyond the gates of cruel Peking,
Your matchless courage shall a nation sing.
Ye dared to speak your mind, to do your deed,
With simple probity as life-long creed;
And e'en in death, oh surely, do ye gain
A worthy goal for lives so free from stain.
Of tireless vig'lance, trusty to the core,
Your fame, enshrined within a nation's lore,

Shall stand, as stand the hills around your home—
The far-famed hills, now famous for your tomb;
Entwined in hearts, like eddies on the mere—
Whose bowing sedges drop the trembling tear.

Ye left us but a hundred days ago,
And ye are gone indeed! Those days must grow
To thousand autumns ere ye come once more.
We bow a last farewell, and humbly pour
Our cup of simple wine before the bier—
The ancient pledge of fellowship most dear—
Recalling all the converse of the past:
The genial words and smiles from first to last.

Now, merged with glist'ring stars will ye remain;
While we, alas, grope on 'mid storm and rain.

Why should not judges get riches, as well as those
who deserve them less?—*Samuel Johnson, Boswell's " Life,"* 1857, p. 245.

Gentleness of manners, an engaging address, and an
insinuating behaviour, are real and solid advantages, and none but those who do not know the
world treat them as trifles.—*Lord Chesterfield's
" Letters,"* cxv.

Fine words and an insinuating appearance are seldom
associated with true virtue.—*Confucius, " Analects,"* Book I., chap. iii.

CHAPTER IX

WE have now to consider that "lord mayor's show" of urchins with red boards, an umbrella-bearer or two, evil-visaged lictors *ad lib.*, and the great sedan-chair, which we saw, in glaring incongruity to all surroundings, passing along the Shanghai Bund. Had we met it in the streets of any Chinese city, it might have appealed to us as containing some elements of barbaric splendour, albeit of a shabby-genteel kind, and we can imagine that amid such surroundings, and to Chinese eyes, it might appear quite imposing. But here, along a macadamised road, with trees on one side and three-storied edifices on the other,

amid 'rickshas, carriages, and well-drilled
police, it was manifestly barbaric with the
splendour left out. Which means—and a
significant fact this—that Western civilisation reveals the incongruities of mandarindom.

One authority on China has hardly
been quoted in these pages, the Empress
Dowager. It would only be gallant to
allow a lady of such dignity to have her
say on a subject which she has made a
life-long study.

On the general subject of the old
economy, including the institution of mandarindom, she said (Imperial Decree,
November 13, 1898): "As the Empire
has always prospered under the old *régime*,
and the methods of old—inaugurated and
sanctioned by the sacred ancestors of our
dynasty—have attained the acme of excel-
lence, there is no necessity for making any
changes. . . ." While with regard to the
case of individual mandarins, she said

(July 18, 1899) : " Bearing in mind the corrupt and dishonest conduct of officials, which . . . has lasted for years, . . . we repeatedly urged upon our Viceroys and Governors the duty of exercising prudence and care in the selection of honest and proper men as sub-prefects and district magistrates, who would earnestly strive to cleanse *the dishonesty and corruption prevalent in the yamêns.* . . . We now remind them of their duty to be continually on the watch to prevent dishonesty and extortion within their jurisdictions. . . ."

From this we should gather that, though the mandarin system is excellent, many individual mandarins do not in their general conduct exemplify the excellences of the system ; though even the latter point seems to be debated by Chester Holcombe (*The Real Chinaman*, 1895, chap. x.). Must we venture to differ, and with most Europeans, and with, perhaps, three hundred million Chinese to support our verdict, say that although mandarindom is about as corrupt an institution as can be, various individual mandarins are exceedingly respectable and highly-respected men ?

There lies before me on the table an annual land-tax paper, which had to do with one's own premises in China. It is marked in the plainest figures (an equivalent of) 30 cents Mex., and was bought as a receipt from the collector for one dollar thirty cents ! The collector was an unsalaried financier, who needed what proportion he could retain from hungry *yamên* underlings of the odd thirty cents, and the difference between the remaining dollar and the thirty cents marked on the paper would go to the county mandarin, who is practically an unsalaried man, having for his recognised stipend a sum comparable to that claimed in Shanghai by an average house-boy, a sum which would not cover the salary of the mandarin's secretary, not to mention the hundred and one paid or

unpaid *attachés* of his *yamên*. Besides
this, however, a county mandarin is allowed
about £100 per annum, as a " save-face " or
anti-extortion sum. But even thus, in the
book of the law of mundane necessity it is
written, " Mandarindom doth not live by
taxes alone," even though a county mandarin may, as a matter of custom, pocket
twice the amount he hands on to his
superior the prefect, who of course makes
like deductions before he hands the rest on
to the next higher official—who does the
same. The Chinese phrase for an upright
mandarin is one who does not drink the
well-water of the district without paying
the populace for it. But how can the man
live? His proclivities for a neighbouring
well may not be very pronounced, especially
if he has read up any translated work on
zymotic diseases and sewage contamina-
tion. But however upright his intentions,
he must get a living somehow or other.
And as he has expended a large sum in

what we should vulgarly describe as buying his preferment—a sum probably loaned by various friends—he must make money, at any rate to the extent of that amount. Then, his expenses with superior mandarins are great. Apart from all ceremonial presents, every case of a criminal condemned to death, being handed on from the county court to the prefectural *yamên* and upwards, costs the county mandarin over $1,000, or £100, in "stationery expenses" alone. So that, if some criminal cases are a great expense, he must do his best to make money out of civil cases, and accept at least the proffered "presents" from both plaintiff and defendant.

A Chinese scholar enters the toils of mandarindom with some respect for the conscience-stirring maxims of Confucius, but how can he possibly work out those maxims in practice? Daniel might remain alive for some hours in a den of unfed lions, but we can hardly imagine him taking up his permanent abode there, and for the miracle to be prolonged indefinitely. His bones would surely be picked clean before many days had passed. And they are few whose Confucian conscience can remain alive and robust year after year in the lions' den of mandarindom. It has been affirmed that no mandarin in office could well be a Christian. Is there not also a mutual exclusiveness between the moral (as distinct from the political) system of Confucius and mandarindom?

Should we not have more than a shadowy parallel between modern China, were he whom the Chinese call the Master to suddenly appear in the flesh, and old Judæa, when He whom we call Lord did appear in the flesh? For the mandarin is Pharisee in ceremony (Sadducee in creed), and Publican in practice, rolled into one. And there is little doubt as to the treatment that mandarindom would mete out to Confucius, were he to revisit his old haunts in northern China once more.

" But 'tis their duty, all the learned think,
 T' espouse his cause by whom they eat and drink,'

as Dryden reminds us.

While we agree with the celebrated Han Yü, of the T'ang dynasty (A.D. 764–824), that "were it not for the Sages, (Chinese) mankind would have perished long ago "— perished, at any rate, in regard to things admirable—our wonder is that, with the cancer of mandarindom preying upon the body politic, China has not perished long ago.

The explanation is simple, however. The nation has lasted under numerous modifications for the reason that its millions of populace have lasted, and because there has been no nation near at hand which has been big enough to absorb China. But its "break-up" under rival rulerships has happened, for a while at least, not once but often. Changeless China! It has changed mightily in political aspect every second or third century since the days of Confucius. Yet, as a French statesman quoted by Herbert Spencer says, "Empires fall, Ministries pass away, but the Bureaux remain." That has been the one changeless element.

But just as the bulk of a Chinese city may often be found outside the city walls, so the chief part of the actual government of China is carried on outside the mandarin's *yamên*. And it is the unofficial government in the little clan-circles, by the village head-man, or the local schoolmaster, arbitrators and peacemakers—the latter appearing in couples at every quarrel —which has been the prop of every dynasty and the saving of the nation. Although, on the other hand, mandarindom is largely responsible for that love of peace which is ingrained into the Chinese nature, for litigation may often spell ruination, perhaps to both parties.

While the mandarin gains his position

from a literary style based upon the Confucian writings, and therefore utilises Confucianism, and also feels that "those systems which teach about heaven and hell (Buddhism and Taoism) are a help to governing, and make up for the lack in the efficiency of the rewards and punishments" (*vide* Diary of Marquis Tsêng), and therefore utilises these also, what is there in Western civilisation or intercourse that mandarindom can possibly utilise? The people have rebelled times without number against the extortions of mandarindom, and will any sort of education, imported from lands where mandarindom is unknown, make the populace more submissive to extortion, however much the missionary may exhort his converts to be good citizens and respect the powers that be?

As Wau Sing, a Chinese banker in Chicago, once said to a reporter, "The advance of the so-called civilisation! I hate every step of it!" so mandarindom is groaning all the time. For the "rise of the people" and its own continued existence are manifestly incompatible; it means their rising before long once and for all against mandarindom. The one man who may very reasonably be scared at the Yellow Peril is surely the mandarin.

"For should Western influence spread through China, as a ride in our sedan-chair along the Shanghai Bund assures us to be highly probable, then are our days numbered. And what of our vested interests?

"Then that great red-brick Customs building in the centre of the Bund for all to see, representing a conspiracy of the Westerners whereby, on receipt of a definite salary, the whole of the proceeds go out of our mandarin cash-boxes to the Imperial Government!—shall we in time have to bow to the popular demand and learn from the barbarians, so as to come down to that?"

And a voice from the blue makes answer, "Yes, or *go!*"

At Rome especially, the national religion was simply
and solely self-adoration. This was the idol
which received more incense than all the gods
of Greece.—*Pressensé.*
The Chinese Empire, with its feudal ranks and its
conservative institutions, is itself the object of
Chinese worship.—*Geo. Matheson.*

CHAPTER X

It is not impossible that the title of the present chapter may evoke a mental conversation between certain readers and the author, as follows :—

"Æsthetic pigtails!"

"Nay. Rather the land where the pigtail is objected to on æsthetic grounds."

"Then you do not refer to 'The Land of the Pigtail?'"

"Strictly speaking, no."

"Thought you meant China."

"I do."

In China the truth always lies a foot below the surface. One must never generalise on the obvious there. "The Land

12   161

of the Pigtail " is a traveller's generalisation. There was once a land to which the
epithet might have been more safely applied.
It was the land in which a distinguished
gentleman once exclaimed, " When a man
loses his queue, his head should go with
it "—a sentence emphasised with an oath
which was considered to be neither im-
proper nor impolite in those days. In that
land the pigtail was once adopted as an
æsthetic adornment, and to this day is
enshrined in the national art. The speaker
was Sir William Fairfax, father of the
famous mathematician, Mary Somerville.

The phrase " Land of the Pigtail,"
stripped of all porcine suggestions, would
properly indicate Manchuria. And not a
few Chinese, watching the rapidly revolving
kaleidoscope of events, have begun to
prophesy the passing away of the Manchu
dynasty, and to look upon their cranial
appendages as a mere fashion of the day.
For two hundred and fifty years, following

the anarchy of eight rebel armies, has the pigtail been forced upon the Chinese nation, to hide from the conquered the fewness of their conquerors. But two and a half centuries count little in a land whose definite history goes back nearly three thousand years, and where time is regarded much as we regard space in this age of steam and electricity.

In not a few homes there are cherished histories of the fidelity of ancestors who, in their attachment to distinctively Chinese modes of dress, chose to suffer the loss of their heads rather than submit to the behest of the Manchu innovator. The Taiping rebellion of reversion to type is not such a very distant event; and then the queue was discarded by millions.

On æsthetic grounds the literati all object to the queue. It is found in no painted portrait or work of art. Barbers are not allowed to compete for degrees until the third and fourth generation, and are thus classified with the degraded classes in company with rascaldom of the most pronounced type. Doubtless political reasons have weighed much in bringing this about, but the ruling instinct among the literati as such has been the æsthetic. And this has affected the importation of many a custom from abroad.

Buddhism has prospered in China, according to Marquis Tsêng, owing to the fact that "the works on Buddhism translated into Chinese, from the excellency of their literary style, appealed to the educated section of the community." He forgets that Buddhism was opposed by the literati for a full thousand years, and at the end of that time had hardly the hold upon China that Christianity has gained after a mere half-century. But it is a fact that not until the gleaming hill-top temple and its vesper bell had entered into the poems of the nation did Buddhism gain a real hold upon the educated section of the community. And toward this result the Buddhist adoption of the most æsthetic flower of China doubtless helped. "My favourite flower is the lotus," wrote a scholar of the eleventh century. "How stainless it rises from its slimy bed! How modestly it reposes on the clear pool—an emblem of purity and truth. Symmetrically perfect, its subtle perfume is wafted far and wide; while there it rests in spotless state, something to be regarded reverently from a distance, and not to be profaned by familiar approach."

From of old there have been two gates in the great wall of Chinese exclusiveness. One is called Utilitarianism; the other and grander is called Æstheticism. And China through the ages has been ruled by scholars whose whole bias (apart from the vulgar utilitarianism of £ s. d.) has been on æsthetic lines. The chief value of the Confucian writings, did scholars express what they feel, lies nowadays in the highly æsthetic manner in which the sage and his disciples have expressed themselves, and in the fact that by studying and approaching the same æsthetic style, the gates of mandarindom are supposed to open to every poor scholar.

The written characters of the "sacred sage" are in themselves works of art, and that on lines of composition which every Western artist would accept. *Making a picture* may be the popular conception of the artist's task; but *the æsthetic grouping of given elements* is the higher principle in the artist's mind. And studying any fine specimen of Chinese caligraphy from his own standpoint, a British artist would find all his unwritten rules of mass-grouping illustrated. It is no necessary reflection on Chinese pictorial art which ranks a well-written inscription higher than any but the finest pictures of China. There are reasons for it which are most apparent to those most fully initiated in universal principles of art.

From the characters themselves it is an easy stage to the grouping of characters into harmoniously balanced sentences. " Tell us a tale " is the popular appeal to the artist everywhere. " Let it be a true tale " add some. " Let it be a thrilling tale " say others. But the artist feels that he is first and last an artist. " Art for its own sake " is his motto, and all else must remain a distinctively secondary consideration. If his art lie in the region of written narration, one set of readers may vote him dull, and another set may vote him a liar. He cares for none of these things ; his narrative is high art, and art-wisdom is justified of her children.

A Chinese scholar once brought me a wonderful series of maps of the province of Kiangsi. The map-drawer had gone on a special pilgrimage through every county in the province, and had drawn these valuable maps from actual survey. That

seemed promising, although the price asked
would have strained the resources of any
but the wealthy. With almost reverent
care the precious bundle was unrolled,
and though prepared for something very
Chinese, the result might well surprise
any one accustomed to Western map-work.
With the fine touches of a miniature painting, the artist had drawn a bird's-eye view
of each county upon a separate square of
white silk, lining out the mountains in
delicate gold tracery. Each square was
a treasure; no lover of the beautiful in
decorative landscape but would prize such
artistic creations. But they were land-
scapes in poem, not maps. As well mistake a Turner painting of any given scene
for an accurately proportioned coloured
photograph of the actual place as call one
of these a map. And so with the Chinese
official narrative of any given political
event. Who could make such a mistake,
except an unsophisticated Western journa-

list (if such a being is to be found in this twentieth century)? Whatever be the accurate account (say) of the tragedy of 1900, or anything else in which " foreigners " are concerned, be sure the official account of that occurrence does not embody it. Turner the glorious a mere photographer! Shades of Ruskin, the thought is barbaric!

As the classics of China have given such a high place to the æsthetic proprieties, those proprieties have long since been regarded as belonging to the highest realm of things sacred—as sacred to the literati of China as was the Temple to the Jews. True, there may be no Shekinah glow within, but " consider the Temple, how it is adorned with goodly stones and offerings." The scholar's national pride and the mandarin's vested interests gather around that Temple. " Is the Temple forsooth to be trodden underfoot of the Gentile foreigners? Is it to be dismantled until there shall not be left one stone upon

another? Missionaries do reverence Confucius, employ Confucian scribes, and with
their aid produce books in whose verbiage
the æsthetic proprieties are observed. But
the mine-prospector and railway engineer
are different. They do not even learn the
colloquial language!" And partly from
these considerations it comes to pass that
(as the Tientsin correspondent of *The
Standard* once pointed out) " the only railway in (north) China—the Peking-Taku
line—runs over a road worked by missionaries for twenty years before it was found
possible to build it; and directly it was
attempted to make lines where the missionary had not paved the way there
was trouble, and the railway stations were
the first things destroyed." And the
stations referred to were destroyed at the
behest of the æsthetic mandarin.

Much further education of the utilitarian
instinct must take place, or else force from
afar must be applied, before such a desecra-

of the national Temple can be endured.
The Jews, with all their traffic in the
Temple courts, would have been humbled
exceedingly before they would have allowed
a subway to a railway station to have been
constructed within the Temple enclosure.

As it is, the one point of appeal which
the missionary has (apart from the renova-
tion of popular manners) is that a Christian
civilsation is the sole means of escape from
the tangled net of China's national sorrows.
And this, indeed, was the last message of
the heroic Tan Tze-tung to a mandarin
friend before he went up to the capital to
die in 1898. But as for the literati
generally, their Confucian training has
lifted their heads too high for them to
see the needs of personal salvation; the
long-established system of mandarindom
has made bribery and corruption in the
law-courts to seem almost Confucian; and
conscience is bound into the benumbed
condition of the women's " golden lilies."

But bringing as it does a higher utilitarianism for the realm at large, many a Chinese scholar is turning to Christianity with half-glances of admiration on that account—inviting it into the courtyard. As a preliminary, the missionary is assured, to its taking possession of the inner shrine of personality and character.

In his *Stones of Venice* Ruskin depicts the attitude of the lovers of the old ways towards the new and vigorously growing Protestantism. This on the one hand, and " on the other stood or seemed to stand all beloved custom and believed legend; all that for centuries had become closest to the hearts of men . . . long trusted legend, long reverenced power "—in which long vested interests may perchance have been incorporated. And thus stands the Chinese scholar of to-day at the parting of the ways. He would like to pull back the clock-hands of the centuries, but sees how the Manchu Court failed to do so in 1900—a more

tragic year for Manchu prestige than for
Western lives. He dare not try and repeat
the experiment, even were he ferociously
inclined towards the " ocean men." He
sees that the times are moving, and that
if he himself may not have to move much,
his sons must. Necessity compels and
utilitarian considerations invite. But alas
for the unique æstheticism to which he
has so long been wedded!

Proud land ! what eye can trace thy mystic lore,
Lock'd up in characters as dark as night ?

CHAPTER XI

THE TRIPLE LANGUAGE OF CHINA

THE unique difficulties of the Chinese language has been a theme for many a writer. And on the other side there is an article in existence "On the supposed difficulty of Chinese," in which the writer (Alfred Lister) makes bold to say, "I maintain that, all things considered, it is an easy language, easier than French, German, or any other European language, and that it can be spoken fluently after a shorter period of study."

The bewildered novice may naturally ask which view is the correct one. And the answer is, Both. Let us explain this at length.

The term "Chinese language" may refer to either or all of three things : (1) Colloquial Chinese ; (2) a written dialect based upon that colloquial ; (3) the literary language of China. And the last-named is exceedingly difficult to master.

Mr. Lister's remarks were made upon the colloquial language. And they would seem to be justified from the fact that missionaries are in the habit of preaching and teaching within a year of their arrival in the country ; while some have launched forth as public speakers at the end of seven or eight months. And these early effusions are readily understanded of the people, although the vocabulary of the speaker will necessarily be somewhat meagre.

What difficulties colloquial Chinese presents, apart from its unrelatedness to any Western language, lie chiefly in the fact that each word should properly be uttered in a certain fixed tone. We are accustomed, for instance, to utter the last syllable of a question in a rising tone. But to do so in speaking Chinese, might turn the final word of a sentence into something quite different from what we intended.

Taking the " tones " of Mid-China for the moment—and they vary in different parts— let us imagine ourselves listeners to the following conversation (with due apologies to the Japanese nation):

" Hi! Are you a Jap? "

" A Jap! "

" I mean a Japanese gentleman."

" I am."

The exclamation " Hi! " would naturally be uttered in a high even tone, which gives us Tone 1. The querying word " Jap " would be uttered in an ascending tone, which gives us Tone 4. The shocked rejoiner would naturally be uttered in a low and slightly ascending tone, which gives us Tone 2, and not to draw too fine distinctions, Tone 5 also. And in the

13

final reply, the word "am" would be uttered in a firm descending tone of voice, which gives us Tone 3.

Now the word for "smoke" has by rights to be always uttered in a high even tone (number 1), and "salt" should always be mentioned in a low tone (number 2); "eye" should be uttered in a firm descending tone (number 3); and "satiated" in a fairly high ascending tone (number 4), although in English all four words would be simply written *yen*.

This at first looks sufficiently forbidding. But in practice, most of these monosyllabic words are coupled with others which, apart from the correctness of "tone," effectually prevent misunderstanding. Thus "water-*yen*" or "dry-*yen*" can only refer to tobacco as smoked in the water-pipes or dry-pipes; "*yen*-iris" can only refer to the eye; and "*yen*-reject" can only refer to satiety or nausea.

As a fact, fewer ridiculous mistakes are

made in colloquial Chinese by the learner than in any other language. If he give the wrong tone—and some never master the right ones—the impression conveyed is that he is from another part of China, where the tones differ or may even be almost reversed. So that the tone element need form no formidable barrier to the learner, however wanting in musical " ear " he may be.

To the question as to why the Chinese should differ from all other nations in requiring fixity of tone with every syllable, the reply is that apart from such a method of ekeing out the actual sounds of the language, the extreme paucity of such sounds would create a great difficulty, there being hardly more than four hundred differing sounds in use anywhere, and in the region of Hankow hardly more than three hundred.

Apart from the tones, the simplicity of the language will be readily apparent when it has been explained that there are no

inflections, hardly any plural distinctions,
and that as a fact the most illiterate native
never makes a grammatical blunder, there
being no grammatical rules which he could
break.   Of course this extreme simplicity
may itself be a hindrance to the learner,
but by entering the kingdom of Chinese
as painters have (emotionally at any rate)
to enter the kingdom of art, and versifiers
the kingdom of poesy—" as a little child,"
the simplicity of the language becomes an
undoubted element of ease in the acquire-
ment of Chinese colloquial.   Most Chinese
sounds are at one time or another uttered
by infants the wide world over.   And little
children just learning to speak will imitate
not only the sounds but the tones also of
words given them to repeat.   So that
Chinese, especially in the softened syllables
of what are called the "mandarin speaking" districts, is indeed most literally

> " the simplest form of speech
> That infant lips can try ; "

and becomes simple and easy to the learner as he learns to unlearn, and to renew his youth once more.

What is called " Mandarin " Chinese (or the Court dialect) is spoken with little variation by three-fourths of the Chinese nation, and by all mandarins wherever they may be stationed. It is the language of China, with the exception of the southern coast provinces from Shanghai eastward to the borders of Annam. These southern dialects, however, represent the more ancient sounds of the Chinese language : the purely Chinese populace having been driven southwards by successive inroads of the Huns and Tartars, just as the Britons were anciently driven by successive invasions to the west of England.

Three hundred millions of the Chinese will understand each other's speech with little difficulty, but meeting a man belonging to the remaining hundred millions of the south, they will be dealing with a semi-foreigner, and have the same difficulty in understanding him as a modern Spaniard might be presumed to have in dealing with an old Roman.

So much for the spoken language of China. The remaining divisions of the subject concern the written language, whether based upon the colloquial of any given part, or common to the whole of educated China in a literary style based on the ancient classics.

The Chinese characters are veritable hieroglyphics, being originally so many picture signs engraven on stone, and still redolent with much sacredness in the Chinese estimation. The original signs for sun, moon, mountain, water, and others are very identical with those of Egypt, and the earliest signs for horse, ox, sheep, deer, tree, grass, fish, boat, carriage, differ from the hieroglyphics of Egypt merely in subject and not in kind.

It may be naturally objected that in no

modern Chinese character can be found a likeness of anything in the heaven above or in the earth beneath. The explanation is that while originally composed of graceful curves, the Chinese hieroglyphics became early engraved upon thin slips of bamboo, where the grain would be exceedingly unsuitable for circular strokes but very suitable for angular gashes, and that the ancient ideographs became thus modified to suit the new conditions of engraving. Then when the brush-pen was introduced in the third century B.C., with silk in place of bamboo, and paper following silk, the brush-pen still held the traditions, and imitated the strokes found in the bamboo records.

To understand the difficulty of learning the Chinese characters, imagine yourself in the midst of a community of two thousand folks to whom it is your duty to be introduced, and after introduction to remember the name and status of each for ever after-

wards, and you have the requirements for
reading the simplest book in the Chinese
language fairly represented.   For Chinese
characters are like men's faces in conveying
little or no hint as to their names.   Having
learned to recognise a few to start with,
the manifest family likenesses may help
the learner to make guesses now and then.
But only to guess—and often the guess,
however ingenious, may be very wide of the
mark.   The only available plan is repeated
introduction till the name seems to look out
of the face in question, and one instinctively
knows this person or this character to be
called White or Black, Brown or Green,
Hill or Field, and so on.

But even then the difficulty is not over,
for certain Chinese characters, like certain
human characters, have one or more *aliases.*
"One man in his turn plays many parts."
Gladstone may be statesman and Homeric
scholar, theological apologist and woodcutter all in one.   And so with many a

Chinese ideograph according to circumstances.

Two thousand characters is, of course, a
minimum estimate, although a full knowledge of that number will form a passable
stock-in-trade for a start. The translated
New Testament contains 2,713 different
characters, the whole library of the thirteen
classics, 6,544; while the sum total of
orthodox characters in the Chinese language
amounts to 40,919. It is refreshing to
learn that no Chinese brain has grasped
them all, and that when one of the finest
scholars in the realm was complimented
upon his wonderful prowess in hieroglyphic
lore, he replied with much sincerity—

> "Not many I know, 'tis true,
> But I know how to use those few."

In the *Nineteenth Century* of February,
1900, Mr. Joseph H. Choate propounded
" a new and startling proposition " under
the name of " Harmonic Literature," by

the application of which each word should give or suggest a chord of meaning, as in musical score. And his paper, with little adaptation, might pass for an able description of literary Chinese and its effects upon the reader's mind.

Dr. Martin, of Peking, has described Chinese as "a language of stepping-stones," affording scope for the leaping imagination. And no greater contrast to the exceeding terseness of literary Chinese than some passages in early Hebrew literature could well be imagined. Whatever date Higher Critics may ascribe to such a paragraph as that of Numb. ix. 21–23, where fifty words are used in the Hebrew Bible to explain that the movement of the tabernacle followed the commandment of the Lord, every one must agree that the clause in question was produced when writing materials were cheap, and probably by a people familiar with the use of papyrus, or at any rate parchment.

But in China the gist of the whole would be expressed by five characters : " Tent following command moved stopped." And some of these five characters would furnish a " chord " in themselves ; as, for instance, the sign for *command*, which consists of a stroke and a man (one person), a seal and a mouth (the signed and sealed utterance of one person proclaimed vocally).

Then to later literary Chinese must be added the element of allusiveness. In poetry especially it assumes the reader's intimate acquaintance with numberless classical sentences and historical occurrences. In this respect it may be paralleled by one or two lines of Milton, if written without capitals or line-divisions : " In hesebon and horonaim seon's realm beyond the flowry dale of sibma clad in vines and ealeale to the asphaltic pool." But even thus its obscurity to the uninitiated is hardly re-presented, for we at once guess which words are names of places, as we might not were we to read : " In stronghold and in double caves fortress realm," and so on.

Yet such is the only literature recognised by the literati of China. And just as every guest who calls upon a mandarin must do so in dress-coat and a sedan-chair, so every guest for the literary faculties must appear in the approved fashion, or be regarded as intentionally insulting, like the man at the Oriental marriage feast who appeared among the guests without the wedding garment.

The absence of punctuation marks has already been alluded to, and is felt to be a difficulty at times to the most accomplished native student. But instead of commas and full-stops there are a number of characters introduced into the text itself. These are called " particles," and supply a sort of internal punctuation. They are like the sergeants and corporals which, though taking their places at intervals in the line, do to the careful observer divide up that line into sections.

These sections are properly short ones.
In literary Chinese, as in social feasts,
everything is cut up into easy mouthfuls.
The basis of the Chinese sentence is usually
four characters. Thousands of choice four-
character phrases may be culled from early
writers, to lend a touch of literary piquancy
to a modern composition. And one of the
arts of the modern essayist is to introduce
as many as possible of these gem-like
crystals into his mosaic-work. Thus
describing an impracticable enthusiast, the
hyperbole " feeding on clouds, sleeping in
the moon " might be employed, and for the
utterly besotted or thoughtless the phrase,
" Living in intoxication, dying in a dream "
would be appropriate.

Another characteristic which the above
specimens introduce is that of parallelism.
The genius of the Chinese language and
thought is that of a broad dualism. Something hanging on each side, " to make the
balance true," is a felt want among all

classes, from the burden-bearer with his
pole to the sentence-moulder and the
philosopher. In matters religious it rather
assists the Chinese imagination than otherwise to have two sets of idols—one Western
(Buddhist) and another native (Taoist),
and for the votaries of both cults to hope
to find their way, on the one hand to the
" Western Paradise," and on the other to
the " Nine-storied Heavens " immediately
overhead. In regions æsthetic this instinct
lies at the basis of our musical " harmony "
and " counterpoint." And whatever rules
of pictorial art are now out of date with us,
such as the " three-light " rule observable
in many of the older masterpieces of landscape painting, or the " pyramid composition " so plainly exhibited in such paintings
as Wilkie's *Blind Fiddler*, the element of
subtle parallelism remains and will always
remain. It is found in nearly all ancient
literature, and seems to be based upon a
law of æsthetics rather than the *rule* of any

passing fashion. Well-poised parallelism is the germ of a Chinese poetic style, and there is little literary Chinese prose which is innocent of this adornment.

The final characteristic of Chinese style with which the patient reader will be troubled is that of rhythm. A sentence in the first Hebrew Psalm reads literally: "And in His law doth he hum day and night." For whereas we are accustomed to peruse our books in silence, the Orientals hum or chant theirs, as every resident in China is aware—sometimes only too painfully. This requires that literary Chinese should consist of rhythmic prose adapted to chanting, like the clauses of our own anthem-prose.

If in style, so in subject-matter, Chinese literature must resemble the classics, These to the Chinese mind are crammed with ideal moral philosophy. And although æsthetic musings upon Nature and social intercourse, the higher emotions of friend-

ship and the exhilarations of the wine-cup
are stock themes for poetry, all literary
prose must have a professedly high moral
purpose. Every one of the literati must be
a moral philosopher, whether, in the words
of the Sage, he is "born so, or has learned
to be such, or has laboriously struggled into
the ranks of the learners."

From the above considerations it will be
obvious that there is no opening for the
writer of light literature in the realm of
Chinese prose as generally defined. For
in that realm all are in "holy orders"
assembled in Convocation with solemnised
hearts. Fiction of the purest nature, and
written with undoubted genius, is summed
up in the one phrase "trifling talk," which
being adequately translated, means *trash*.
"A celebrated Western writer of trash has
fallen ill, and Western Emperors have sent
their condolences," was the Chinese newspaper account of the illness of Rudyard
Kipling in 1899.

Before the Chinese Hall of Moral Literature hang boards bearing the legend, " No idlers admitted," and every novelist is regarded as an idler in this Realm of Lofty Purpose. Cant may and does enter the Sacred Convocation, and priggishness is everywhere found therein, but novelists—avaunt!

Not that the literati do not purchase and devour the works of their various novelists, even those which are written in the semi-colloquial style, but these things are done on the sly. Yet as bookstalls are on the increase in all the large centres of modern China, we may devote a chapter to examining their contents, merely adding here that as Chaucer unfolded some of the possibilities of the English language, so there have been novelists in China, some of them almost comparable to Chaucer in the matter of dramatic portraiture, who have helped to develop a popular-literary dialect, based upon the " mandarin," which shall be understandable by natives of most of the eighteen provinces.

14

William of Malmesbury picked up his history, from the time of Venerable Bede to his own time, out of old songs.—*Aubrey*.

> Nought is more honourable to a knight,
> No better doth beseem brave chivalry,
> Than to defend the feeble in their right.
> *Spenser*.

Men will always be what women make them; if, therefore, you would have men great and virtuous, impress on the minds of women what greatness and virtue are.—*Rousseau*.

CHAPTER XII

THERE is a Chinese work of two centuries ago, known as *The Household Treasure*, consisting of twenty - four volumes of double-distilled goody-goodiness. Within its covers, however, is a little section devoted to humorous tales and tales which are meant to be humorous, from which we will quote a motto-anecdote for the present chapter.

A certain musician once went into the street carrying his harpsichord of delicately sweet sound, and commenced to play thereon. Thinking they heard a lute, of somewhat questionable associations, a large crowd gathered to listen ; but, finding that the instrument was the æsthetic harpsichord, they quickly dispersed. One man alone remained, and the musician comforted himself, saying, " At any rate I have one appreciative listener." But the man to whom he referred dashed his fond hopes by exclaiming, " That's my table you are using ! You don't suppose I should stay if it weren't, do you ? "

The obvious moral is that while vested interests may account for apparent absorption in the higher refinements of Confucian proprieties — see previous chapter — something more piquant must be devised to tickle the attention of the masses.

At the very bottom of the list of popular Chinese works, we must notice the ballad booklets, cheap and nasty as regards paper and printing, and containing subject-matter to correspond. Their undoubtedly vicious influence, however, lies in their suggestiveness to the Chinese mind, for the few specimens examined contained anything but

realistic portrayal of badness. Whether
a more extensive study of these booklets
would modify one's verdict is hard to say,
for although Lord Macaulay in one of his
essays urges that no literature which has
influenced the manners of a given generation is beneath the attention of the student,
we beg to be excused such a research in the
case of ballads which every decent Chinese
is ashamed to be caught reading.

Booklets which from their outward
appearance might easily be mistaken for
those just mentioned, contain the standard
plays of China, and may be bought and
studied with interest. Their composition
dates from the tenth century onwards, and
they deal with historical events which were
ancient in those far-off times. To some
Western readers of Chinese they may
appear dull and worthless. The reason
may be the lack of " a certain art in
reading " them. As Lubbock says of
reading generally, " we must endeavour to

realise the scenes described "—in this case so meagrely—" and the persons who are mentioned, to picture them in the Gallery of the Imagination." Especially may this art be acquired when some of these meagrely-worded plays, when acted, draw sincerest tears from the eyes of the crowd around the rough platform-stage.

One of them, abounding in pathos, is published in quarto, from the translation of Sir John Davis, under the name of *The Sorrows of Han*. It describes how a very lovely maiden, whom the Emperor first saw in a dream, was at length discovered and brought to the palace, in spite of the wiles of a faithless Minister; then the wedded bliss of the Emperor (Yuan Ti, B.C. 42) and his consort, until, by the traitorous efforts of the same faithless Minister, she was demanded and carried off by a Prince of the Huns, but cast herself into the Heh-lung river rather than pass the limits of her native land.

A popular amplification of the story is current, which seeks to compensate for the tragic end of the real story by representing a younger sister of the victim, and her counterpart in beauty and virtue, becoming the Imperial consort in due course. Without being maudlin in sentiment, this latter version of the story contains over fifty synonyms for weeping or wailing !

Another pathetic story which has been dramatised is that of *The Statesman and the Woodcutter*, a favourite story indeed in Mid-China where it is located, and " a story to shed tears over," as some of the readers of the English translation have remarked. Such a translation forms a chapter in my *String of Chinese Peach-Stones*, and, as was afterwards discovered, had been already rendered into English by " L. M. F.," under the title of " The Broken Lute," in *The Far East*, 1877. On making a pilgrimage to the grave of the woodcutter in whom the high statesman recognised a soul-fellow, the writer confesses to have felt such emotions as would have been called forth had the wild roses that were plucked therefrom grown upon the grave-mound of a personal friend. And one of the foremost musicians of England has expressed the emotions which the story evokes in no measured strain.

The Chinese themselves have kept that lowly hill-side grave in repair for nearly twenty-five centuries, and have enshrined the memory of the woodcutter youth in their poems and phraseology the wide empire over. Every use of the expressions " sound-knower " and " heart-knower," which we have rendered into English as soul-fellow, is an understood reference to this humble hero, whose intelligent appreciation of sweet music commended him to the statesman-musician, until the twain became "weddyd brethren," as the old English phrase has it.

A still earlier story, dating back to

Davidic days, forms the subject of a play
entitled *The Prince Seeking a Counsellor*.
And a much-read expansion of the story,
The Making of the Gods, was written by
a scholar of the former half of the seventeenth century, to provide the wherewithal
for a dowry for his second daughter.
A certain philosopher, who proves to be
an utter failure as street huckster and no
better as angler—for his rod had a straight
needle at the end and was held above the
water—being discovered pursuing the latter
occupation, formed a cunning counsellor to
a noble Prince at a time when the nation
was groaning under the misrule of Neroic
savagery. But, having slain his country's
foes, this counsellor endeavoured to appease
their ghosts by making so many deities of
them, and they have held rank, according
to Taoist mythology, as spiritual protectors
of the realm, ever since. Truly a choice
specimen of mental topsy-turvydom this!
A Chinese speaker at the Chicago Par-

liament of Religions made bold to say:
"The pity is that Western people only
follow Protestantism and Roman Catholi-
cism and have no true teacher of Taoism,"
and the decadent religion which he advo-
cates is fain to find its deities among the
underlings of the worst tyrant that China
has ever seen!

For the popularity of such objects of
worship, *The Making of the Gods* seems to
be largely responsible. Truly the novelist
is, after all, a national factor in China!

With a passing note of appreciation of
the many excellences of a work called
The Divided Kingdoms, a popular expansion of the national records of the centuries
around that of Confucius, we may next
notice a semi-veracious chronicle of a century of anarchy and confusion—the Chinese
Wars of the Roses—in the second and third
centuries of our era. This work, in twenty
volumes, known as *The Three Kingdoms*,
with nine other works current in the earlier

seventeenth century, was singled out by a celebrated editor and critic and dignified with the epithet, " Work of Genius."

As to its make-up, and that of lesser works since, W. F. Mayers says : " In every historical novel we recognise one unfailing round of personages—the wily and favoured counsellor, the plain-spoken but unvalued minister, the sovereign, either founding a dynasty by martial virtues or losing a throne by effeminacy and weakness, the priest with flowing robes concealing a repertory of magic arts, and, finally, the truculent champion, a compound of Hercules and Bombastes, who brandishes sword and lance and club, all of enormous size and weight, like playthings, occupying half the work with his challenges and encounters. . . . To these ingredients add legendary marvels *ad libitum*, miraculous appearances of the gods in times of need, tricks, treacheries, murders, and banquets, and the romance is ready made to hand."

The T'ang dynasty (618–907) next furnishes quite a small library of romances, all apparently written some centuries ago. No traces of genius may be discerned in their pages, but of their immense popularity as text-books for tea-shop orators much might be said. And it is from this functionary of the Chinese " public-house " that the masses learn the history of China. No ancient sage and no modern statesman is so well known to the masses as one or two of the heroes of these romances.

Test the matter by catechising a coolie on the subject. Ask him, " Who was Hsieh Jen-kuei? How much could he eat? How much could he lift?" and so on; and, astonished that a foreigner has really discovered the obvious A B C of historical biography, a bright thought will flash across his intellect. He concludes that you, like himself, have heard that name from your babyhood, and exclaims, " Yes, of course, he went to your foreign parts, did

he not ? " And we begin to wonder whether
English history of the middle of the seventh
century may not, after all, be somewhat frag-
mentary, omitting as it does a visit from
the most illustrious of ancient Chinese
heroes to our humble shores.

But memory comes to our rescue, and
we recall the precise facts of the case—
according to the Coolie History of China
(Authorised Version). Having received an
insult from Korea, not England, the Emperor (Kao Chung, r. 650–684) burned to
avenge it in person, but the land route to
Korea being then unknown—to the novelist
—and the Emperor being mortally afraid of
sea-sickness, might have merely vented his
rage upon his cooks or housemaids or his
statesmen or a wife or two, had he not been
smuggled into Korea without knowing it!

Problem for Scott, Jules Verne, and
Punch—How to convey an Emperor and
his army from Cheefoo to Korea, without
the Emperor knowing that he was travel-

ling at all, still less that he was travelling
across the briny deep! Could Western
genius successfully grapple with such a difficulty? I trow not. Yet the novelist makes
light work of it—on paper. For at the
suggestion of the immortal Hsieh, a wooden
city was constructed upon a gigantic raft,
the Emperor invited on board, and although
particulars of navigation are wanting, he
did thus actually get to Korea without
knowing it, as every coolie in China knows,
if we do not!

The Southern Sung dynasty (1127–1280)
gives rise to one or two unimportant works
of fiction. And the founding of the Ming
dynasty (1368) has furnished us with an interesting account of the illustrious Emperor
Hung Wu, who rebuilt the city of Nanking
on such a grand scale, with walls thirty
miles round, whose gates have no need to "lift
up their heads," however high the banners
of the entering hosts may wave. The story
is only slightly mythical, and agrees with

the orthodox historical records in tracing
the rise of the hero from a famine-stricken
childhood, then cow-boy, then Buddhist
novice, then leader of a band of young dare-
devils, then commander of the insurrec-
tionary forces, until success makes the
insurrection a revolution, and Hung Wu
ascends the Dragon Throne and founds the
Ming (or Resplendent) dynasty.

But matters do not stop here, and the
dismal sequel has to be chronicled. The
woes of his grandson and the fermenting
germs of dissolution fill the concluding
chapters of the book.

This brings us to the Manchu conquest of
China (1644), which, together with the
prowess of Wu San-kuei, a faithful general
who did his utmost to preserve China for
the Chinese, although he had to call in a
Manchu tribe for that purpose, and so failed,
has also given rise to a work, which, however,
is tawdry in execution and unworthy of the
occasion.

Such is a fairly complete list of the historical romance literature of past centuries in China. But the last decade of the nineteenth century has produced a work of fiction which for bulk and quality may bear comparison with any previous specimen of light literature. An exhaustive analysis of its contents will be excused when it is explained that it contains a full million characters, while the English Bible contains but 773,746 words, and the Chinese literary-style Bible but 676,827 characters. Which says much for its quality and fascination, else what publisher would have accepted it?

In point of style it may be said to well-nigh exhaust the possibilities of the " popular-literary " language, and in general tone it is as robust and healthy as some Chinese novels are the reverse. Its writer is both a genius and a gentleman.

The title of the work may be rendered *A Noble Brotherhood*, and the heroes which

give it such a name form a class of knight-
errantry unknown in Western literature.
For they combine the qualities of detectives
with those of a very chivalrous knighthood.
They may often appear in the guise of
the "night-scouting thief," and were they
devoid of the virtues they happily possess,
would be formidable pests to the community
at large. But possessing all the capacities
of the most skilful burglar, being adepts at
wall-scaling on dark nights and the like,
they become, in all their fertility of strata-
gem, veritable warrior angels for the succour
of the oppressed, as they are a roving
Nemesis for the oppressor.

The book abounds in elaborate stories of
the *Sherlock Holmes* order, and even Conan
Doyle might not scruple to recognise the
author as a companion genius in that particular form of literature. And to come to
the climax of one section of the work, what
Western novelist would first amalgamate
the knight and the detective in one, and set

15

him at work to steal the most sacred item of the crown jewels from the forbidden precincts of the imperial palace, and by a complicated scheme of personification secrete them in the house of a highly connected villain, then get a junior accomplice to come forward and declare through thick and thin, before the severest and keenest-witted judge that China has seen, that it was indeed stolen three years before by the keeper of the regalia, and that he saw it brought to the house where it was found; and yet through all the trickery and perjury involved in the scheme, to conserve the higher requirements of that truthfulness to inner fact which far transcends the mere truth in word—to smash the shell, and yet preserve the delicate kernel intact?

Two specimens of miscellaneous literature may next be noticed as being procurable in every Chinese bookshop. The *Liao-chai* book of marvels, with which the English reader may become familiarised in the form of Prof. Giles' *Strange Tales*, is the first of its class in point of style and also of date. It is a chosen recreation for literary lovers of the weird. And another mode of escape from the rutty high-road of Confucian admonition is found in a collection of ghostly and ghastly tales entitled, *What the Master did not talk about*—meaning "Extraordinary things . . . and spiritual beings."

A Jekyll and Hyde story within its covers might well have suggested that piece of English literature, had R. L. Stevenson been a Chinese student as well as the novelist he was. Moreover, the story is accompanied with an explanation that is logical enough from the Chinese point of view. The Chinese Jekyll (a resuscitated corpse as it happens) was in possession of both his higher soul (*psyche*) and his lower animal spirit (which we may for the moment call his *animus*), the latter being under due control from the former. But as the "dead man" continued talking to his friend, his *psyche* gradually evaporated, and his residual *animus* became a criminal animosity which sought to murder his friend. And only a speedy flight and the leaping of a low wall averted the tragedy.

Thus Jekyll is seen to be *psyche* plus *animus*, and Hyde to be *animus* minus *psyche*. Which simplifies matters wonderfully; and also explains why Chinese mothers so often stand at the door of an evening and call to the spirit of their little one, who has evidently lost it—being "not himself at all." If "not himself," what is he? Why, *animus* minus *psyche*, of course!

A popular work may next be mentioned as casting all conventionality to the winds, and exhibiting the spirit of higher morality in one who was notorious for neglecting the letter of the laws of decorum. It is known as *The Drunken Demigod*, and deals with the career of a high-born youth who happens to be a re-incarnate *Lohan* (*arhat* or Buddhist saint), and who by and by awoke to self-consciousness. Refractory as a novice, he becomes an apparently mad monk and a winebibber, and acts in the wildest and most questionable manner. There is, however, a divine method in his madness, and his inner motives and outward achievements furnish an adequate reply to all questionings. Things are not what they seem, and his saintship becomes fully recognised at last.

His vagaries recall to mind a certain St. Symeon Salos whose history is given by Baring Gould. Symeon's claims to canonisation, however, are on a par with those of Nero to fame as a benevolent personage. Young Nero wept as he signed his first death-warrant, and Symeon began well—so well, indeed, that the perusal of the first chapter of his life-story decided the saint-seeking readers to recommend him to the Holy Pontiff. Accidents will happen! and he whose day of homage is July 1, and

whose full history might better suit Chinese
print than English, is dismissed by the
orthodox hagiologist, Alban Butler, as follows
(the comments being those of Baring
Gould): " Although we are not obliged in
every instance to imitate St. Symeon, and
although it would be rash to attempt it
without a special call; yet his example
ought to make us blush"—*we should think
so, indeed*—" when we consider"—*ah !*—
" with what ill-will we suffer the least things
to hurt our pride." Of the two, we ourselves
are inclined to prefer the drunken demigod,
for he always stopped short within an inch
of transgression, other than drunkenness.

Then we have one or two collections of
short stories, the best of which are included
under the title of *Wondrous Narratives.*
The story of *The Statesman and the Woodcutter*, contained therein, has been already
noticed. Another story in this collection
is that entitled, *Fanning the Grave.* It
is given by Goldsmith in his *Citizen of*

the World, 1763 ; in Davis's *Chinese*, 1845;
and in Professor Douglas's *Chinese Stories*,
1893.

It now remains to notice the love-tales
of China, in which the human heart has
to grapple with the limitations of Chinese
custom, as well as with the problems that
oppress true lovers in Western regions.
In all of them, Cupid calls one way and
parental arrangement or social circumstances the other.

The earliest of Chinese romantic novels
dates back to the fourteenth century, and
as the lighter literature of China was
then to be found in dramatic form, that
form is assumed in the work before us, an
operatic love-tale known as *The Western
Annex*. A widow and her lovely daughter
take up their lodgment with a rogueish
waiting-maid and serving-lad in the un-
occupied western wing of a large temple.
A young graduate enters the temple
grounds, and decides from a glimpse of

one of its inmates to lodge there also, in another set of apartments. His emotions do not diminish thus. And it is quite a privilege for him to have the honour of rescuing the others from an attack of brigands; in reward for which services he receives the promise of the maiden's hand. The danger over, however, mamma remembers to forget him, and only through the waiting-maid can he send his literary and verbal effusions to his true love. At length an interview is arranged, whereupon mamma waxes wroth, and sends him off to the capital to take the highest degree if he can, which being acquired, she consents to the ratification of his secret marriage.

Such is the plot of a little drama which has been included among the ten "Works of Genius," and is now issued with a lengthy introduction and copious laudatory commentary by its scholarly editor of the seventeenth century. That it shocked the taste of many is evident from a sentence in the preface, " Some have come and said that *The Western Annex* is a bad book. Such slanderers shall assuredly be hurled into the tongue-cutting hell. . . . It is an inspired work of genius. . . . To the bad it will appear bad; to the pure it will prove itself an inspiration."

Another poetical romance has been rendered in lineal translation by P. P. Thoms at Macao, 1824; partially transcribed in verse by Dr. Chalmers, 1867; and wholly in prose, with copious notes, by Sir John Bowring, 1868; the latter under the name of *The Flowery Scroll*. It describes how a brave young man is betrothed to a maiden he has never seen, and in love with another whose charms he knows better. He goes off to the wars, and is "killed." Whereupon his faithful affiancée calls herself a widow, and "commits suicide by drowning." This is sufficiently tragic, but we rightly suspect that neither of the two may be quite so dead as they are reported to be, and anon find the hero returning from the wars with glory. And now, as his betrothed is "dead," he, with the Emperor for match-maker, marries the other one. When lo! his dead betrothed appears on the scene.

Would any Western novelist bring such a complication to a satisfactory end? The Chinese author does so very easily, by making the hero marry both—and more wonderful still, by making all three live happily ever after.

Another such double marriage forms the climax of another work, translated by Professor Julien as *Les Deux Cousines*, which can be read in English on reference to *The China Review*, vol. i., in a lecture entitled, "An Hour with a Chinese Romance," by Alfred Lister, who describes the work as "the best, all things considered, that I know."

Another novel, also of the seventeenth

or eighteenth century, is that known as
The Fortunate Union, translated by Sir
John Davis, but having previously been
rendered into French as early as 1766.
And another, translated by Professor Julien
as *Les Deux Jeunes Filles Lettrées*, in
which two pedantic young ladies and two
scholarly youths rival one another in
producing elegant pieces of prose and
poetry.

Of more general interest is *The Galaxy
of Heroes*. The little son of one official
family is betrothed to the infant daughter
of another, and having reached a marriage-
able age, is despatched to claim his bride
from her father, now Governor of Shantung. On the journey thither, however,
his treacherous servant robs him and leaves
him apparently dead, then proceeds on his
journey to personate him before the
Governor of Shantung.

Our hero meanwhile is discovered by a
gallant young hunter, and slowly recovers.

Meanwhile the young lady, finding that the suitor is of low and mean disposition, refuses to marry him, and feeling assured that he is an impostor, disguises herself in male attire, and, with a faithful attendant, flees to Wuchang to make inquiries of her suitor's mother.

Finding that his daughter has fled, the Governor resolves to hush up the matter, and palm off an ugly waiting-maid upon the false suitor, who is paid out as he deserves. And the right couple get married at last, after a due amount of adventure.

And now we must notice a famous novel which Mayers declares to be, " beyond possibility of cavil, a work for which genuine admiration may be expressed," that most quoted of Chinese tales, *The Dream of the Red Chamber*. With Mayers' verdict, however, some have ventured to differ, notably the writer of an altogether unique review of the work, in *The Chinese Repository*, 1842, who actually mistakes the hero for a

" very petulant woman " ! More reliable renderings of the story have appeared from the pen of Mr. Thom, Sir John Davis, and Dr. Edkins as regards part of the work, and by Mayers and Professor Giles as regards the whole — the latter sketch being still on sale.

The author is supposed to have been secretary to an hereditary grandee of the eighteenth century. That household was Manchu, not Chinese, and so undoubtedly are some of the characters and scenes described. The chief character is a spoilt boy, whose disposition is hardly improved by his spending his later teens in the almost exclusive company of his two maiden cousins and their waiting-maids in a sumptuous household. To one of the young ladies he is bound by predestination and by elective affinities. She is of great beauty, but so is her cousin also, and being of delicate health and of a sensitive nature, is constantly driven to despair by the attentions that the spoilt youth bestows on her good-natured but rather stolid rival. By and by the parental powers that be betroth him to the latter maiden. Where-upon his true love pines away and dies. He marries the other against his will, and on the fortunes of the household col-lapsing he becomes a Buddhist monk.

Such, in barest outline, is the plot of one of the most remarkable works China has ever produced, and with only that plot before us, we may

"Grieve for the senseless youth, the hapless maiden's woe."

And that the author intended to call up such emotions, and perhaps give vent to a pessimistic view of the course of true love, impeded as it is by mundane circum-stances, seems to be implied from the fact that the line of verse above quoted is part of the dream in the " red chamber," during which a fairy instructress endeavours to initiate the hitherto gay and thoughtless youth into the realities of life; in which task she is seconded by a faithful waiting-maid, who now and then urges upon the youth a course more in keeping with his position than the indolent and effeminate one he was adopting.

To the student as such, the book abounds in material for his philosophisings; to the lover of a skilful portrayal of the finer shades of human emotion under ordinary and in abnormal situations, the work is unparalleled in the whole compass of Chinese literature; but to the young Chinese novel-reader, such a book will form anything but wholesome diet. And we can well understand why, apart from the disclosure of family secrets — and the writer evidently drew from the life—such a work should have been proscribed by the authorities for fifty years after its publication; that it should have been again proscribed in the thirties (when MS. copies sold for as much as £7 or £10), and that it should be proscribed at the present moment. With the result that it can be bought everywhere under the innocuous *alias* of *The Stone Records*.

Let a man of the present age go back to the ways of antiquity;—on the persons of all who do so calamities are sure to fall. — *Confucius, " Doctrine of the Mean,"* xxviii. 1.

CHAPTER XIII

AMONG the edicts put forth to check the modernisation of China after the *coup d'état* of September, 1898, was one decreeing the abolition of the native newspapers which had sprung into being in the chief Treaty ports of China. Its text may be given as illustrating the attitude of the Manchu Government toward what have come to be considered by us of the West as so many daily necessities, and their editors, well, as fairly respectable men according to our barbarian estimate of things. Let us, however, own our ignorance, and consent to be instructed by one who has ranked higher than any Son of Heaven which the Court

227

of Cathay has produced for some decades. She says :—

" As newspapers only serve to excite the masses to subvert the present order of things and the editors thereof are composed of the dregs of the literary classes, no good can be served by the continuation of such dangerous instruments, and we hereby command the entire suppression of all newspapers published within the Empire, while the editors connected with them are to be arrested and punished with the utmost rigour of the law" (Imperial decree, October 8, 1898).

On this *The North China Herald* naturally remarked: " If we may liken the effect of the Japan-Chinese war to a severe electric shock administered to China, we may also speak of the native Press as a telegraphic system conveying an electric current of new ideas throughout the length and breadth of the land. To cut off this current, to which the nation has now become habituated, is a crime and a stupidity which is worse than a crime. The Empress Dowager is like Mrs. Partington with her mop; the tide of enlightenment is flowing in China, and if she and her friends at Peking had a little more knowledge of the world, she would know that her edicts cannot possibly stop the rising of the tide."

But her helplessness was displayed in a manner which the Western reader, unaccustomed to ways and means in China, would hardly guess. For most of the newspapers have continued from that day to this, as though no edict had been issued. There would be two possible ways of achieving this result. One would be to subsidise the mandarins of the neighbourhood. And the second, which was the method adopted, would be to add a foreign name as proprietor on the front sheet, thus placing the newspaper under foreign protection. And this latter method is in vogue in many another enterprise than that of journalism. The avidity with which many a Chinese capitalist or merchant has availed himself of Western protection against the extortions of the Chinese mandarin system is indeed one of the prominent signs of the times in latter-day China.

Of the score of Chinese newspapers which survived the drastic edict for their suppression, one of the highest class is that which we may call *The Daily Mirror*, keeping back its real name for reasons connected with a leading article which we propose to translate later on in the chapter.

The *Daily Mirror* arose out of the Reform Movement. The reformers first started a paper which, out of pure compliment, bore the same title as that of the Christian Literature Society's famous monthly, *The Review of the Times*, a magazine dealing with national questions in the light of Christian civilisation, started in 1868 by Dr. Y. J. Allen, whose name has long since been a household word with most mandarins and leading scholars throughout the Empire. As identical titles would naturally lead to confusion, the native *Review of the Times* became *Chinese Progress*, and flourished till the Usurpation. After that *coup d'état*, the editorial staff divided and threw their energies into two rival papers, one published every ten days, the other, the daily paper before us. In order to save itself, it disowned the now disgraced K'ang Yu-wei, and trimmed its sails in the approved Chinese fashion.

It is printed on foreign paper and published at about a third of a penny, having risen from a farthing, and gives good value for the money. The outside sheets are, of course, a mass of advertisements. Taking up a copy at random, let us first glance over these essentials of a paying daily.

Under the bold-print title, we find, beginning from the right-hand top corner, rates of advertisement, then items of surpassing interest in the current number, then a

marionette show " patronised by royalty "
in Siam, &c. ; edible birds' nests, expensive
but of prime quality ; Wuchang Cotton and
Silk Mills ; an artist's advertisement ; an
advertisement of another artist far superior
to the former; life insurance ; fire insurance;
fuel ; cigarettes ; weighing machines (illustrated) ; a Chinese drug-shop where Western
medicines may be obtained (as sundry
Mission dispensaries have found, for it is a
reliable institution) ; and lastly lead type.
And the back sheet is in no wise inferior to
the front in the number and variety of its
advertisements, comprising as it does an
illustrated announcement of a circus ;
Peacock brand cigarettes, also illustrated ;
and a host of other delights for the Chinese
mind and body.

On looking within, we cannot but be
struck with the high journalistic ability
therein displayed, both as regards the wide
range of reliable news from all provinces
and many countries, and as regards the

vigour of the articles which that news calls forth.

In the news section, we begin with the latest Imperial decrees, transmitted by telegraph, then translated telegrams from the British press of Shanghai—so that our London telegrams are in the Chinese reader's hands within twenty-four hours, as a rule, after we have read them at our breakfast tables. Such names as Dreyfus, Rhodes, Lord Salisbury, Chamberlain, Lord Roberts, Lord Kitchener, Kruger, De Wet, and others, have been well to the front at various times. And all the leading national or diplomatic events are portrayed, together with condensed reports of our own Parliamentary debates on Eastern questions, with an accuracy which leaves little to be desired.

Russia has never been popular with our editor. He has long prophesied that whatever events befall, she will be coming out top of the pile, with enlarged territory, at Chinese expense, in the end.

Then as to domestic news, a Chinese statesman or Western ambassador falls ill, and receives a paragraph; a Consul becomes betrothed to a " female friend," and the date of his marriage is duly reported. The state of the crops, from the borders of Tibet to the opposite extremes of the realm; the prospects of the silkworm industry; the decline of the tea-trade, and the fact that Ceylon tea may now be bought in Hankow; the decadence of Chinese art in the potteries, and the like, are duly noted and form topics for articles too. The ravages of opium are dealt with, accompanied with an array of facts and inferences which might well surprise the Opium Commissioners of a few years back. A forbidding tax on opium lamps is proposed in one of these vigorous leaders: statesmen of the first and second grades should be made to pay one thousand taels (ounces of silver), of the third and fourth grades, five hundred taels; of the fifth, sixth, and seventh grades, two hundred taels; of the eighth grade downwards, fifty taels; the upper class civilians, thirty taels; the middle classes, ten taels; the lower classes, three taels—an amount which will be appreciated when it is explained that these latter would hardly spend a penny a day on food. The rates for the higher classes are lower in proportion to their income for the reason that when a man can afford to feed well, the effects of the opium-grip may be palliated for a much longer time. And the article ends by quoting a friend of high degree who says: " Such a method needs to be commended to Court to regulate the self-poisoning of the masses, and should such an edict be granted, first taxing and then prohibiting, the populace will be rescued, and in twenty years' time the realm will be free from opium. But will the realm indeed enjoy such a con-summation? Ah!"

And now it is proposed to translate a political article of some years back, in which we have the spectacle of enraged patriotism, while yet certain events were fresh. It may be well to say by way of introduction, that while it mirrored the general feeling about the loss of Kiao-chou, certain facts on the other side are understated ; that the translator has no feeling of animosity toward Germany, but the reverse; that no anti-German article will reappear in *The Daily Mirror* ; and that in the " holy land " of Shantung—the birthplace of Confucius, the region which contains the sacred T'ai mountain, and is the province where the maximum of friction would be supposed to have been caused—on January 17, 1901, the Governor of the province cordially invited all Protestant missionaries to follow the missionaries of Germany and France, and return to their posts in the interior, officially promising them a military escort if needed, full liberty of worship for their converts, and all the aid in his power toward furthering their own " preaching of righteousness "—a translation of which document may be found at length in *The North China Herald*, January 30, 1901.

With such a preface we may safely quote *The Daily Mirror* leader of April 19, 1899 :

" CHINA SHOULD PREPARE FOR WAR, AND FIRST FIGHT GERMANY.

" Present-day China is like unto a broken tile, or a pile of eggs ready to tumble ! And those who sorrow for her misfortunes moan saying, ' If we fight we are lost, and if we do not fight we are still lost ! ' But to Court and country, I would say, ' Tell me not that in either case we are lost. I will not believe it ! Let us fight if only to wipe out our national disgrace. And we must begin with Germany. Why ? Because the ' slicing of the melon ' (partition of the country) began in the mind of Bismarck [!] , and its first violence was marked in the siezure of Kiao-chou. And now Germany is planning to seize I-chou—fearless of con-

sequences and careless of every principle of
justice. Thus of all nations, Germany is
the most insulting and overbearing. Alas!
alas! that such seeds of dissolution as
these should be sown; while the Terrestrial
Empire looks on with indifference! Surely
no Empire worth the name would do so.
Avert dissolution! Fight! And begin with
Germany. Consider the rights of the case.
The German usurpation of Kiao-chou was
only made on the grounds that some villains
had harmed some missionaries. Did not
the German Government know that our
Empire has laws against villainy? Must
they adopt lynch-law themselves? Have
we no methods of dealing with criminals?
Did the case prove that China had none?
They might have been justified if we had no
such methods, or if those methods had
failed. And all the while our Government
has been straitly charging the officials
everywhere to put down villainy with vigour,
and to protect all strangers within our

borders. Why must they use military force
and seize our territory ?

" If China had turned a deaf ear to
arbitration, and had cast aside her treaties
[As she did in this and other cases.—TRANS-
LATOR], there might have been some excuse.
But they must fight a hurried battle and
make a military matter of it. They must
win ; we must lose, and agree to resign our
territory, and that without having violated
any treaty whatever ! They just regarded
us as Barbarians who own no ruler, and
with whom they could do as they pleased,
being, as they boast, a civilised nation and a
powerful Empire ; and impose upon us as
having no freedom like their own ! Thus it
was that they could do as they liked, and
cast justice to the winds ! And we tamely
submitted !

" Germany's usurpature of Kiao-chou was
not only an insult to our Parental Emperor,
but to the whole realm of Terrestrials ; and
not only to the men of the present day but

our ancient Monarchs, Yao, Shun, Yü, T'ang, and to our diademed Confucius. And our Government and Magistracy cannot ' pillow the lance ' and brook the outrage. Rather must we memorialise the Emperor to collect his troops and avenge the insult, an insult which proves the Imperial reliance (upon Germany's faith) to be unfounded, and which takes advantage of the sorrows of the populace. And if officials and people talk about ' present danger,' ' threatening crises,' and the like, they will indeed prove themselves to be a herd of enslaved Barbarians, who may be hunted and hooked like so many beasts and fishes. Then I too will join in the cry, ' If we fight we are lost, and if we do not fight, we are still lost ! '

" But surely we must utter bolder words than these ! Listen, I beseech you. There cannot be more than a thousand German soldiers at Kiao-chou, and in the event of a battle will every one of them escape ? And if they lose but one to a hundred of our

troops, or ten in a thousand, or a hundred
to a myriad, can they slaughter our whole
army ?

" Moreover, their recent doings have been
an insult to every Terrestrial, and Germany
should find in every Terrestrial soldier an
enemy. If our four hundred millions rise
in opposition to Germany, will there be any
fear of our failing to conquer the foe ?

" There are Western methods of warfare,
but have we not learnt them ? There is
Western discipline, but has no one adopted
it ? If the Government will not withhold its
treasure for rewarding bravery, are there no
heroes who will answer to the call?   We *are*
able to fight then.

" Can we not make guns and cast cannon,
and protect our frontiers from foreign occupation ? We are able to protect ourselves.
What fear we then?

" And after this I-chou episode, if we do
not arm *en masse*, ' turning our backs on
home, and joining as one,' I guarantee that
17

the melon will indeed be sliced. With all our myriads we shall bow our greetings to these guests ; with all our mineral wealth, we shall submit to the conquerors.

" China must fight, and fight now ! And if the National resources are inadequate, the populace will help ; civilian households will supply rations to the troops ; the mines will supply material for armaments. We are able to overcome Germany, I assert for the second time.

" If we put on a bold front, though the Germans have taken Kiao-chou, we shall be host and they guests, we shall be masters and they servants. And should they want to collect reinforcements of men and weapons, their country is distant ; and if they seek to borrow troops on the spot, what nation will assist them? Our country is broad and large, the united forces of a dozen provinces could be concentrated in one province, and that without undue pressure on the populace, or the expenditure of for-

bidding sums of money. We can concentrate, yes, concentrate the soldiery of a
dozen provinces, and oppose this one kingdom. We need not cross the seas to collect
the sinews of war as they would have to.

" When France attacked us, and ' defeated
our horse-tails ' at Foochou, were our troops
seized with panic ? Did not the provinces
of Kwangtung and Chekiang rise to the
occasion and prove their prowess ? That is
no distant event. Is it utterly forgotten ?
And now with Germany, cannot such things
be repeated ? We are able to overcome, I
assert for the third time.

" I maintain that at all costs ('body
and bones ground to powder '), we should
struggle to be free from the slavery of
driven cattle. The Government should not
be affrighted at any recent defeat (in the
Japan war), but should adopt a policy of
lasting victory, by immediately proclaiming
throughout the Empire that Shantung must
be held in order to secure the safety of the

remaining provinces. If the military spirit of a myriad mile territory be concentrated there, the Germans will fear and fly without having the nerve to resist. We can thus conquer without fighting ! Bold words these, but as true as they are bold. We are able to overcome Germany. Who doubts it ?

" You may say that China is divided in heart, and if we organise a great army, we shall find the country people scattered like a flock of frightened birds. But will it be so ? The insult to one country in Asia is an omen for all Asia. And we need not debate matters with Westerners. Other nations are willing to help, but cannot till we invite them. But if our Government were to make representations of our national disgrace and ignominy, and ask for aid of our friends the Japanese [!] and others, and Japan and Siam were to realise that China's disgrace was Asia's danger, then every Asiatic power would be likely to unite in a common bond to withstand

Germany and escape the tyranny of the White Race. Thus the East would join in war against the West, and China would be ruled by its own laws and belong to its own people. And so with each (Asiatic) nation, as justice requires. And with such available help from related nations, Germany would be defeated. China can fight and save herself, and the plan of national salvation is (chiefly) to arouse the literati and populace to feel the shame of the foreign yoke, thus uniting the nation in one, and the Continent in one. But first the nation must be united as one body where every part feels the pain of one part.

"The literati and populace of the Empire should form one council of war, and call out volunteers to make up for the paucity of regular troops. Eastern Asia should form an Asiatic council of war; every man in every part should exert himself to save his home.

"If our Government but feels anxious for the realm, and our statesmen are but shamed at the national disgrace, the populace will catch their emotions and weep tears of blood. Public spirit will be aroused. Our friends the neighbouring nations will fight for their very existence, and when the conflict comes, there can be no possibility of our not being victorious.

"Alas, the insurgents (the Germans) are insurgents indeed. How could I remain silent, and not address my country? And doing so, how could I refrain from speaking plainly, and appealing to our Far Eastern friends (Japanese and the like)?

"But, after all, the matter belongs to our Government. If the Government gives the word, the drum-beats will resound throughout the Empire, and reverberate in every manly heart till the martial spirit rises wave upon wave.

"Otherwise, if we dawdle in our extremity, and are blind to our calamity; if we delight to be destroyed and count our losses gain, then all is lost, all is lost! China is China no longer. Alas! Alas! How can I bear it! How can I bear it!"

A passing thought in the reader's mind may be answered at once. It may be argued on reading the above that if the editor has published articles against the Empress Dowager, couched in such terms as those employed against an episode in the relations of Germany with China, she might well suppress such a newspaper with an easy conscience. But as a constant reader of *The Daily Mirror*, one is qualified to assert that not even in 1900, when Chinese no less than Western opinion was roused against her treachery, was one disrespectful word or insinuation to be discovered in the leading articles of this paper, although many a well-deserved epithet was hurled at the heads of certain "vile statesmen" who had misadvised her.

Nor, apart from the above article, has
our editor published much that could be
considered anti-foreign, though he has
penned a great deal that we should readily
admit to be the outcome of a very allowable
patriotism.   And if he should be somewhat
critical of such Western manners as are
not admirable, he lashes the abuses of
mandarindom with a vigour that is nothing
short of courageous, considering that he
has readers among that class of dignitaries.

And even in the above article he cannot
be considered to "excite the masses to
subvert the present order of things," or
even to urge them to attack Germany or
any other Western power, for the simple
reason that his articles, so far from being
understanded of the masses, are in the
finest and most allusive literary prose.
The man in the street could never manage
to punctuate an article in *The Daily Mirror*,
still less read it.   The readers, apart from
the official section thereof, belong to the

ranks of the sedentary student or the educated merchant—both men of peace who would not handle a weapon of warfare for the life of them. So that even this specimen of patriotic rage may well be considered to be as innocent of harm as a resounding volley of blank cartridge. It is a mere artistic beating of the air, and would be chiefly admired on account of its vigorous style.

No effective advocate of militarism is the native press of China, but its more able publications are in many ways an agency of education in the sorely neglected subject of a healthy patriotism such as it would be to the best interests of both Orient and Occident to foster in China.

And as most of the higher class dailies gain their facts from Western journalism, and many of their motives from the publications of the Christian Literature Society for China—a society which includes within its membership many of the most intelligent well-wishers to China, residing either within that empire, or north of the Tweed, or in various cities of England, America, and Germany—we may well regard the daily press of Cathay as an important factor in the new China which is coming to birth with the new century.

And surely we may read the signs of the times as birth-throes rather than break-up. Or as an ancient *Aid to Pleasant Discourse* relates of Adam in an old Mystery Play, so also with China to-day : "As the curtain rose, he was seen crossing the stage on his way to be created."

For EU product safety concerns, contact us at Calle de José Abascal, 56–1°, 28003 Madrid, Spain or eugpsr@cambridge.org.

 www.ingramcontent.com/pod-product-compliance
Ingram Content Group UK Ltd.
Pitfield, Milton Keynes, MK11 3LW, UK
UKHW010342140625
459647UK00010B/771